IDEAS & RESEARCH

Elements of Article Writing Series

IDEAS & RESEARCH

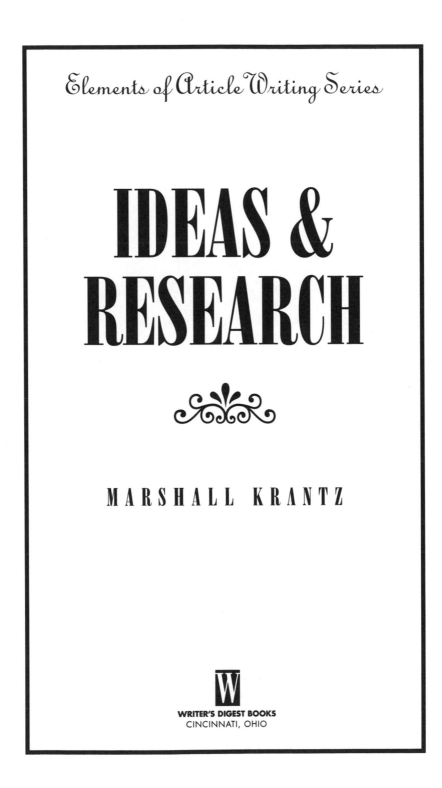

M A R S H A L L   K R A N T Z

WRITER'S DIGEST BOOKS
CINCINNATI, OHIO

Ideas & Research. Copyright © 1996 by Marshall Krantz. Printed and bound in the United States of America. All rights reserved. No part of this book may be reproduced in any form or by any electronic or mechanical means including information storage and retrieval systems without permission in writing from the publisher, except by a reviewer, who may quote brief passages in a review. Published by Writer's Digest Books, an imprint of F&W Publications, Inc., 1507 Dana Avenue, Cincinnati, Ohio 45207. (800) 289-0963. First edition.

This hardcover edition of *Ideas & Research* features a "self-jacket" that eliminates the need for a separate dust jacket. It provides sturdy protection for your book while it saves paper, trees and energy.

Other fine Writer's Digest Books are available from your local bookstore or direct from the publisher.

00 99 98 97 96 5 4 3 2 1

Library of Congress Cataloging-in-Publication Data

Krantz, Marshall
    Ideas & research / Marshall Krantz.
        p.   cm.
    Includes index.
    ISBN 0-89879-718-7
    1. Authorship 2. Research. I. Title.
PN146.K73   1996
808'.02–dc20   95-48338
                                                             CIP

Edited by Jack Heffron and Roseann Biederman
Cover and interior designed by Sandy Kent

ACKNOWLEDGMENTS

Thanks to the writers who kindly consented to being interviewed for this book. Their insights give the book much more depth than otherwise would be the case. Thanks especially to Fred Setterberg for additionally taking the time to share his thoughts on research and to critique my manuscript. Thanks also to Jack Heffron and Roseann Biederman at Writer's Digest Books for their suggestions and careful editing. Last, thanks to the National Writers Union for the support it has given me and hundreds of other freelance writers over the years in trying to survive in a tough business.

TABLE OF CONTENTS

The best nonfiction comes from original research, and the most exciting original research usually comes from the field. This chapter covers the elements of fieldwork: observing people and places, and talking to people.

Don't worry if you can't make sense of your material right away. With the benefit of time, themes and patterns will emerge and the story will become clear.

ABOUT THE AUTHOR

Marshall Krantz has worked as a full-time, freelance writer since 1985. His articles have appeared in dozens of national and regional publications, including *The Washington Post*, *Los Angeles Times*, *Christian Science Monitor*, *Country Home*, *Audubon*, *Diversion* and the inflight magazines of United and Delta airlines. He has contributed to travel guidebooks published by Bantam Books and HarperCollins, and to the travel literature anthologies, *Travelers' Tales Mexico* and *Travelers' Tales Spain*.

INTRODUCTION

Good nonfiction tells its story as vividly and convincingly as possible and at the deepest level of understanding that the writer is capable. This starts with the writer. Why does the writer want to write? What does the writer hope to accomplish? How does the writer define his or her relationship to the marketplace? Within this basic framework, the writer then develops ideas for articles, researches the subjects and writes the articles. Following this logical progression, this book moves from defining oneself in relationship to the marketplace to ideas to research.

The book emphasizes that facts, more than simply defining the difference between fiction and nonfiction, give nonfiction its power to affect readers; facts are the building blocks of true-life stories. The book also gives you a philosophical framework for approaching the prewriting stages of nonfiction along with specific tools and techniques for successfully developing article ideas and gathering information. I've tried to supply ample examples from my own experience and the experiences of other professional writers to illustrate the points I make so you can better understand how theories are put into practice.

These two elements of nonfiction writing, ideas and research, are paired in one book because they are inextricably bound together. Asking which comes first, the idea for a nonfiction piece or the research for it, might seem obvious—the idea—and to a certain extent there is a logical progression from ideas to research to writing.

But it's not that simple. It's a lot like the chicken-egg question. The *initial* idea may come first, but the final idea of a story, what the story is ultimately about, comes at the end, the final touch on the last rewrite, and maybe not even then. Research is in a real sense a search to find out what the story is about. The story may end up not exactly, or even remotely, what the writer started out perceiving it to be. In addition, ideas and research compose an unbroken circle. You must do nonspecific research all the time to get ideas, and research on individual stories leads to ideas for other stories, which leads to more research and more ideas.

I use the words "articles," "stories" and "pieces" interchangeably throughout the book; editors and writers more often than not refer to articles as stories. It's helpful to think of articles as stories, anyway, to keep in mind that your job as a writer often is to tell people stories, because people love stories. Stories are specific and concrete, and therefore the way people best understand the general and abstract. Even when you're writing yet another article about seven ways to lose weight and the story is primarily educational and expository, the article still must engage the reader with specifics tied directly to a concrete reality.

I hope you'll come away from this book with a greater appreciation for research, a much undervalued and underpracticed reportorial skill, and the crucial role it plays in creating strong articles. I also hope to ease the intimidation some writers feel when they must do research; it's easier than you think once you've learned a few basics. Last, I hope to convey my and many writers' enthusiasm for research. For those with a questioning mind (an essential character trait for any good writer), research is the scratch to the itch of curiosity.

And, believe or not, research is fun. Once you start, you may find it hard to stop.

CHAPTER ONE

The Nonfiction Writer, Ideas and the Marketplace

In a very real sense, the writer writes in order to teach himself, to understand himself, to satisfy himself; the publishing of his ideas, though it brings gratifications, is a curious anticlimax.—Alfred Kazin

Sir, no man but a blockhead ever wrote except for money.—Samuel Johnson

Freelance writers must write exceedingly well to make it in the competitive world of newspaper and magazine writing—that's a given. But writing well is only part of the story. Writers must have something fresh and interesting to say for which someone else—an editor—will pay money. And having something to say for which someone else will pay money is no easy task.

Since this book is about how to find ideas and do research for article writing, primarily magazines, and you're reading it, I presume you expect, or at least desire, to publish your writing and make some money in the process; writers who intend to make little or no money from their writing write poetry.

Before you run off looking for ideas for specific articles, perhaps you should begin at the beginning: Define yourself in relationship to the marketplace, and perhaps more important, to yourself and your writing. This raises some basic questions. Like, what kind of writer are you? Or want to be? What kind of writing do you want to do?

What do you want to write about? Perhaps even more basic, what kind of person are you? Or want to be? This first chapter tries to help you answer the first set of questions. For answers to the second set, consult your psychotherapist or spiritual advisor.

Finding a Niche: Specialization

While it's true that the quality of your writing must meet the standards of the publication for which you hope to write, it's also true you're going to have to come up with great ideas *and* convince editors you're the right person to turn those ideas into stories. Editors throw their own ideas only at the most exceptional writers, or writers with whom they've built a relationship. All others have to sell themselves, as well as their ideas, to editors.

The quickest way to convince an editor you're right for the story you propose is to be an expert. Editors want to feel comfortable that you know what you're talking about. And, justifiably so, they want to feel you'll bring a background of knowledge to a subject that others can't, and thus improve the final product, the printed article.

So, in one way or another, most nonfiction writers specialize in one or a few areas to define themselves to editors—before editors define the writers as adding no value to a story and thus pass them over when it comes to making assignments.

Writers can specialize in a variety of ways. They can specialize in a subject, such as health, business or technology, areas which are in high demand, or they can specialize in a conceptual subject, such as change or human desires. They can specialize in their approach to a subject, say, using narrative to tell a good story, or they may rely on style, say, folksy humor or ironic wit.

The point is to define yourself to an editor and demonstrate somehow, with clips of published articles, or your query letter if you have no clips, that you can do—even better, have already done—what you propose to do should you get the assignment.

A specialization, or niche, often generates assignments. Editors with whom writers have already worked are inclined to assign more, similar stories, and editors who don't know the writers personally, but have seen their work, may also contact those writers for specific stories.

Specialization saves a freelance writer time and energy in a number of ways, and considering how hard earning a living as a freelance writer can be, anything that makes life easier is worth embracing.

First, writers who specialize in a specific field don't have to start from scratch with each new assignment. They don't have to consume a lot of time and energy learning about a new field or seeking interview subjects or ferreting out written material. Good researchers can accomplish these tasks efficiently, but writers who have done it before for previous assignments don't have to do it all over again.

Second, writers working within one field can use the same research and interviews for a number of related stories. Freelance magazine writer Andrew Leonard, for example, interviewed the same sources for computer articles about self-publishing on the World Wide Web, interactive advertising and Internet directories accessible online. "I can ask one person a bunch of different questions and use them for three different articles," he says.

Third, research for one story often leads to ideas for related stories. Writers may uncover information while researching one article that suggests another article, or questions that arise about the story they are working on may require a whole other story to answer. Subjects, in a sense, lead writers further and further into a specialization as the writers learn more about their subjects.

Specialization allows writers to stay focused. Trying to think about widely disparate subjects at the same time can prove distracting, and make you better understand, to your dismay, the term "scatterbrained."

So, how does one go about finding a niche? For some, specialization derives from expertise previously gained through a job or avocational interest. For others, the answer involves deeper questions and often much soul-searching. In the stories of writers that follow, you can see the various ways in which nonfiction writers specialize, and how they came to those specializations.

Trading on Experience: Subject as Specialization

Probably the clearest, easiest route to developing a niche is to specialize in a particular topic or field. You can define your specialization as broadly as health care, for example, or narrow it within that broad field to, say, nutrition. You can pick a specialization that interests you and learn it on the job of freelance writing, although an established expertise makes you more competitive right from the start.

Peter Temple, for example, had worked in finance for nearly eighteen years, lastly as division director of a securities brokerage firm in Britain, when the stock market crashed in 1987. Unfortunately, Temple's career crashed along with the market. "I was made redundant," he succinctly puts it.

Despite his hard luck in the business world, Temple was enviably situated to launch a career as a freelance writer: He was a bona fide expert in an area of journalism much in demand.

As a broker, Temple had specialized in the beverage and leisure industries. So he narrowly, and successfully, targeted his queries about the business end of beverages and leisure to trade publications such as *What's Brewing*, *Wine & Spirit International* and *Leisure Week*. He also received a few assignments from national newspapers such as *The Independent* and the *Evening Standard*.

Temple's previous insider status especially positioned him to compete with other freelance writers for assignments at the trade publications, because trade publications, which by definition target people in a specific line of work, demand a high degree of technical expertise for their articles. This demand narrows the competition considerably, although the downside of a narrow niche is fewer markets to which a writer can pitch stories.

But Temple used his narrow niche in trade publications as a springboard to expand his new career. As his journalistic reputation grew, Temple wrote about leveraged buyouts, money laundering, derivatives and investment software for national magazines such as *Professional Investor*, *Analyst* and *Securities & Investment Review*. He has also published two books, *Traded Options: A Private Investors' Guide* and *Self Made Millionaires*.

Temple attributes much of his success to an insider's knowledge of the securities business and the financial world at large.

"I think there was, and still is, a shortage of writers with direct experience of working in the stock market who can also write lucidly about it," says Temple. "Most stock market professionals are addicted to the market and to the money they can make."

Temple's strategy of marketing his highly specialized expertise to the publications that most needed it proved a winning formula. His expertise gave him immediate standing to compete with other freelancers, and he then combined his expertise with his growing journalistic track record to win varied assignments at larger publications.

Pursuing Personal, Public Interests: Issue Specialization

The late Speaker of the House Thomas "Tip" O'Neill Jr. will long be remembered for, if nothing else, his famous political dictum: "All politics is local." A more basic corollary might be: All politics is personal.

For Laura Fraser, writing about women's health issues grows out of her own personal and political concerns. It is, in a sense, an organic expression of who she is and what stirs her both emotionally and intellectually.

After graduating from Wesleyan College, where she was editor of the campus newspaper, Fraser started in the early 1980s writing primarily for publications with a politically left point of view. She contributed to publications such as *Mother Jones*, *In These Times* and an alternative weekly newspaper in San Francisco named *The San Francisco Bay Guardian*.

"I was always interested in feminist issues, and first among them at that time was abortion, freedom of choice," says Fraser about how she began writing about women's health issues from a political perspective. "I did a lot of stories about reproductive freedom issues, which led to a wider range of health issues. All along I'd been interested in how women's bodies were controlled by men and how women have tried to regain control. That includes not only abortion rights but also medical abuses against women and the ways that women view their own bodies and feel that they have power over their bodies.

"The second thing was my own history with weight problems and eating disorders, which fits into a lot of the same issues of who has control of women's bodies. There was also a need [for articles about women's health issues]. There are not that many writers who can ask intelligent questions about the medical establishment and take complicated scientific information and write about it in a friendly manner. So it was a clear niche. Also, there are not that many fields in writing these days where you can make a living and write about things that you feel make a difference."

Fraser now regularly writes for the top women's magazines and is a contributing writer at *Health*. For *Vogue*, she's written about the detrimental effects of dieting, and about a seventy-five-year-old physician who flies from Minneapolis to Duluth to perform abortions because no doctor in the city will perform them; and for *Glamour*, she's written about the abortion pill, RU486, and about botched cosmetic surgeries. She's also working on a book for Dutton about the diet industry.

"Basically," says Fraser, "I think what it comes down to is that you have to write about what you have a passion for. Editors have called asking me to write about skin-care creams or exercise machines, and I'm not interested, not only because I'd be bored doing those stories but also because that boredom would show through in the work. If I don't have an interest and a drive to dig deeper, the story is going to be worthless."

Fraser's passion is fueled by her parallel private and public concerns, and, as she points out, her passion, combined with her skill, produces articles that leave editors wanting more.

Taking Stock: Conceptual Specialization

Some niches are not as easy to figure out as choosing any one of hundreds of subject niches ranging from alligators to zucchini. While a subject niche can put you on a firm footing in the world of freelance writing, there are good reasons to examine niches that span specific topics. In nature, highly specialized animals most often become extinct; the adaptable animals survive. So, too, in nonfiction writing. As previously mentioned, too narrow a specialization can lock you out of other jobs. But just as important to many writers is the freedom to pursue their interests wherever those interests might lead.

Joe Flower built himself a successful freelance career long before he figured out his specialization. A poet by avocation and musician by occupation, Flower lost his job playing guitar in San Francisco Bay Area convalescent homes in the late 1970s. In a fit of what some might call hubris, Flower convinced himself he could earn a living as a freelance magazine writer.

As it turns out, Flower knew his capabilities. He quickly broke into regional publications, though it did take a bit longer to break into the black. He wrote about a wide variety of subjects, including sports and business, mainly because assignments came his way. Before long he had moved on to prestigious national magazines, writing sports features for *Esquire*, travel destination stories for *Islands*, and how to buy a hot tub without getting into hot water for *Playboy*. Although Flower was doing well as judged by the magazines in which he published, it seemed that Flower's subjects picked him rather than his picking them.

"I wrote just about anything," Flower recalls. "I started writing about health care because at the time I was married to a woman who was in the health-care business, so I knew the difference between DRGs [diagnostic related groups] and PPOs [preferred provider organizations]."

While covering health care, Flower profiled Ken Dychtwald, an expert on America's aging population. The profile appeared in *Healthcare Forum* in 1985, and soon after, Dychtwald invited Flower to coauthor a book with him about aging. That book, *Age Wave*, was published in 1989 and sold 250,000 copies. But more than just reaping healthy sales, no small matter in itself, the book created a turning point for Flower.

"Writing that book was interesting and useful," says Flower, "but what really fascinated me was watching Ken, because he had one subject, the demographic shift in America. And from this one subject he had built a thriving career as a writer, speaker and consultant. I could see how having one subject could be very useful to one's career."

Flower decided to do for himself what he observed that Ken Dychtwald had done for himself, but with an important difference: Flower wanted a broader field in which to move.

"I was struck by the thought," he says, "that when you're struggling to build a lead, one method is to look at what you've already written, because it's already there. So I decided that if there was a subject fascinating enough for me to focus on, I'd probably already written about it without realizing it. I sat down one weekend and speed-read everything I had ever published, which at that point was several hundred articles, *Age Wave*, and the manuscript of a second book, which was about Disney and [Disney chairman] Michael Eisner.

"I realized that they all had a great deal in common. It didn't matter whether I was talking to Bo Derek, Muhammad Ali or a shaman off the islands of British Columbia, I asked them all essentially the same question, how had they dealt with change. This was the same approach I took to writing about business organizations. I was less interested in their particular structure, products or personalities than in how they changed over time. I decided to look at my work through that lens and do consciously what I had done unconsciously."

Like his role model, Flower has built a multifaceted communications business, except instead of aging, Flower's subject is how people and institutions cope with change, particularly as it relates to health care and high-tech telecommunications.

In addition to writing articles for magazines such as *Wired* and *New Scientist*, Flower consults, gives speeches, moderates online computer conferences and publishes a newsletter. He has also created a presence for himself in cyberspace. His Change Project is on the World Wide Web (at http://www.well.com/www/bbear/), and his Windom Health consulting firm has been involved with Time Warner in creating a health venue on a full-service, interactive cable system in Florida.

"It doesn't matter to me that I'm not in places like *Esquire* anymore," says Flower. "I'm more interested in writing about my subject from the stance that I'm working in areas where I feel I can make a difference."

Lest you think Flower's noble aspirations have cost him in income, think again. "Since I made that discovery," says Flower, "my own income and ability to get things published have increased markedly."

Flower's experience demonstrates how writers can methodically choose conceptual specializations based on their aptitudes and inherent interests, and demonstrates how venturing into a variety of media, including writing articles, enhances one's reputation as an expert, leading to additional work.

Telling Stories: Treatment as Specialization

The three previous examples of writer specializations deal with subject matter or content, ranging from concrete to conceptual. But some writers specialize according to their treatment of stories, or rather the forms in which they prefer to work. In these cases, content follows form, meaning that writers conceive story ideas that are conducive to their preferred form while excluding others.

Jim Morrison, for example, admits he "bounces" from subject to subject: sports, business, online computer communications, the environment. But while his subjects vary widely, Morrison's approach to those subjects largely remains the same.

"I'm very interested in literary journalism," says Morrison, who contributes regularly to in-flight magazines for Southwest and American Airlines and has also contributed to *Playboy*, *Reader's Digest* and *The New York Times*. "I like to write descriptive narratives, stories that take you someplace, introduce you to characters, try to dig beyond the surface by showing you the story or the person."

Morrison's article for *Southwest Spirit* about how the Mississippi

River flood of 1993 wreaked havoc on one town along its banks, Valmeyer, Illinois, is a case in point. Morrison takes readers to the town descriptively and tells the stories of various townspeople, what happened to them and their homes, and how they and the town have tried to rebuild.

In an article he also wrote for *Southwest Spirit*, about how oyster fishing in Chesapeake Bay has practically ended thanks to pollution, over-fishing and disease, Morrison opens his piece aboard the oyster boat *Stanley Norman*. He describes how the boat's skipper and a Maryland Department of Natural Resources biologist dig through a dredge basket, only to find a sorry catch. The rest of the piece is mainly a more conventionally constructed magazine feature, that is to say, it is structured around conceptual elements that support the article's thesis, but Morrison also works in the stories of other Chesapeake Bay fishers and how their livelihoods have eroded over time.

As you can see, Morrison's articles lend themselves to storytelling. They are not, by contrast, the best subjects for service stories, which generally instruct readers in practical solutions to problems. A writer turning Morrison's subjects into service pieces would write about how to improve oyster fishing in Chesapeake Bay (or perhaps alternatively how to increase development around the bay), and how to prevent river flooding or what to do after a flood. The service treatment is so different that it in effect changes these stories to subjects other than those about which Morrison wrote.

Morrison concedes that not every assignment fits into the niche he's defined for himself. Inherent interest in a story and financial concerns also guide his decisions.

"I am curious about many things, so I often will take assignments that may not fit into the structure for literary journalism. And it's hard to get paid enough to really have the time to do that kind of work."

In that vein, Morrison has written for *BrandWeek* about how Viacom is trying to create brand recognition for itself, and for *The New York Times* about the adhesive bandages football players wear on their noses (to help keep open their nostrils and thus improve airflow).

In addition to the niches writers choose for themselves, editors also place writers in niches, as Morrison points out.

"Often, I find editors define you; you're the writer who can put it together on a tight deadline, or the writer who can spin a good yarn,"

Morrison comments, referring to his own strong suits as editors see them.

Despite his reliance on subject treatment as specialization, Morrison says editors still rely on him to come up with story ideas.

"Occasionally, editors will call me and want to do a story on a pro golfer, and they'll say, 'Find us one,' " he says. "And I also constantly have to come up with ideas on my own. Right now I have twenty ideas out there [circulating among editors]. For a freelancer, coming up with ideas is a job in itself."

Rather than depending solely on his specialization, Morrison combines a handful of "niche" qualities that clearly define him to editors: his narrative treatment of a story, or his ability to "spin a good yarn," as he puts it; his knack for conceiving salable ideas; and the quick, reliable turnaround he can offer editors. These qualities work synergistically to spell success for Morrison.

Styling a Distinctive Voice: Sensibility as Specialization

A writer's voice, that is, the written expression of the writer's personality, makes an article distinctive. And like story treatment, voice is not merely a matter of style, but an expression of a writer's sensibility and contributes to the final determination of what a story is about.

Judith Newman claims she never sought a specialization. "I don't have a scheme or plan," she says, "as a writer this was defined for me." But if you scratch the surface, you'll see that almost from the onset of her magazine writing career she found stories that were slightly askew, a perfect fit for her irreverent way of looking at the world.

For example, Newman ran across people who constructed securities trading floors in Manhattan and pitched the story to the once hot but now defunct, *Manhattan, inc.* The magazine was familiar with figurative "trading floors," the term used to describe the activity of securities trading at an exchange. The magazine and its readers were not, however, familiar with the actual, specially constructed floors on which the trading took place. So for *Manhattan, inc.*, Newman's idea was quirky. In an amusing style befitting a story based on a semantic joke, Newman informed readers about the literal nuts and bolts of securities trading floors.

With that first magazine piece in 1988, Newman found her niche, an amusing approach to offbeat topics. (She'd previously written one newspaper piece, for *The New York Times*; a *Times* editor she knew asked her to write a story about celebrities and their cars.) She contributed regularly to *Manhattan, inc.* and then began querying other magazines. According to Newman, editors liked her style but not her ideas.

"I'd go for slightly more obscure topics," she recalls, "but my queries rarely worked. But it almost always worked out that I got assignments, but not for the stories I'd pitched."

Editors sensed how Newman's individual style and sensibility meshed. (It's important to note she took the freedom to project her absurdist sensibilities into her writing style.) Soon, she was in an enviable position. Editors associated certain kinds of stories with Newman and called her. "Editors sometimes call and say, 'That's a Judith Newman story,' " she says. "I think if editors have hired me, it's because they've seen something I wrote that's funny, or whatever."

Newman's subjects might best be described as loosely fitting into the category of human desires. She has written about a hair colorists' convention for *Mirabella*, facial surgery for *Self*, and a cigarette lighter museum in London for *Forbes FYI*. Her work has also appeared in most of the other top women's fashion and beauty magazines, as well as *Rolling Stone* and *Penthouse*.

It's not true that editors simply feed Newman ideas; she has really set the tone for editors to think of stories as a "Judith Newman story," and she still comes up with her own ideas.

For *GQ*, for example, Newman dreamed up "Sex Machines."

"I was thinking about how cars are sold on sex appeal," Newman remembers, "so I wondered what it would be like to have sex in them. It was a paltry excuse to rent ten great cars and test them with the man who's now my husband.

"I think of an idea that's in the air," Newman explains, "and then put a little twist on it, and write it with my own particular voice.

"I've made lots of money and had fun," she says. "I have a sense of playfulness in my work. Not many people can get up in the morning and say, 'I'm going to write about underwear and write about it to the best of my ability.' There's something to say for that."

A distinctive voice like Newman's, reflecting a distinct way of looking at the world, makes her stand out from the competition and, from an editor's point of view, means the difference between generic copy and one-of-a-kind articles.

Discovering Self: Beyond Specialization

Since at its most satisfying, nonfiction writing is an exercise in self-discovery, it can take a lifetime to find one's specialization, if you define specialization as that thing you discover about yourself. And if not a lifetime, perhaps a mere decade or two, as in the case of Jacques Leslie.

At age twenty-four, Leslie was hired by the *Los Angeles Times* as a correspondent in southeast Asia during the Vietnam War. Although he spent only a few years with the *Times*, the experience of war reporting, and specifically the intense stimulation the war provided, confounded and bedeviled him for years; he had become a self-admitted war junkie.

"Almost any journalist who spent any time in Vietnam felt that other stories lost their significance," explains Leslie. "After I quit, I floundered for a couple of years, and part of it was the depression of . . . the opposite of all that stimulation [of the war]. Eventually my way out of that was to begin writing about it.

"After I finished the first draft, in the early 1980s, I tried to get it published, and I came very close. But to my great relief now I did not succeed. Eventually I wrote seven drafts of the book. I would work on it and put it away for a year or two; get it out, work on it again; until finally I realized the great, stunning epiphany that is now the end of the book: one, that the book had been a vehicle for a search; and two, what the object of that search was. At that point I had completed the process."

The end result of Leslie's process is the three-hundred-page *The Mark*, published by Four Wall Eight Windows.

Reflecting, Leslie says, "I was, after awhile, quite consciously on a search. I couldn't exactly tell you what for, but only later did I realize that it had to do with understanding the nature and source of my attraction to the war. Writing was one way of getting to the bottom of that, although it wasn't the only way.

"I think it is very important for people to honor that part of themselves that wants to undertake that kind of search."

In the pursuit of self-knowledge, more hardheaded business deci-sions, such as a steady income, obviously take a backseat. This form of specialization can result in monetary as well as psychic rewards, but you must decide to brave what in all ways is a riskier venture than a solid, clearly defined and salable specialization.

Specialization: Niche or Pigeonhole

Writers are a restless bunch, mentally. Their curiosity demands the freedom to roam where it will. Which is why many writers resist defin-ing themselves, or worse, being defined, as one kind of writer or an-other, even though a specialization offers some measure of job security in that highly insecure field known as freelance article writing.

To avoid being pigeonholed, writers such as Jim Morrison define their niche in terms of story treatment, thereby freeing themselves to explore a variety of topics. Others, such as Joe Flower and Judith New-man define their specializations in broad, conceptual terms, although they also appear to concentrate their efforts on certain topics: Flower in health care and high-tech telecommunications and Newman on sex and relationships, celebrities and body image.

Newman concedes she feels trapped at times in the niche she's cre-ated. "What's interesting and engaging to me shifts at times," she says. "I love doing celebrity profiles and then there are times when I never want to meet those people again. At times, I want to think about fra-grances and the place they have in our lives, and at other times I don't want to think about them again."

But Newman may be a victim of her own success.

"I'd like to write about medical subjects in a writerly way," she says, pointing to Oliver W. Sacks, the neurologist who wrote *The Man Who Mistook His Wife for a Hat*, as a model. "But if someone calls and waves a large paycheck in your face are your going to say no? Are you going to turn it down for something more high risk and specula-tive? As a freelancer, I feel that I have to accept all the assignments editors offer or they won't call anymore."

Even though Laura Fraser writes mostly about women's health is-sues, she maintains that writers who build a reputation for excellent writing and reporting skills can transcend pigeonholing, provided they come up with good ideas.

"I think at this point," says Fraser, "I have a good enough reputation as a good and thorough writer that I could get an assignment about any fresh idea. I did a piece for *Mademoiselle* about the world women's bodybuilding contest, for fun; I wrote a story about fly-fishing for *Health*; and my story about my interview with Yassir Arafat appeared in the Sunday magazine of the *San Francisco Examiner*. I've found editors to be quite receptive to ideas you wouldn't really think would fit into a mainstream publication."

Testing the Waters

For many writers, it takes awhile to find a niche. Expect—*welcome*—a period of experimentation. Even masters of nonfiction, such as John McPhee, whose long, fact-filled pieces have filled *The New Yorker* for more than thirty years and have produced twenty-two books and counting, rambled around the nonfiction universe before finding his niche. In an interview in *Creative Nonfiction*, McPhee said, "I didn't rule out anything as a younger writer. I tried everything, sometimes with hilarious results. I think that young writers have to roll around like oranges on a conveyor belt. They have to try it all. If they are lucky, they'll fall into the right hole."

Luck helps, sure. But with some critical examination of your strengths and weaknesses in writing and reporting, a clear evaluation of your temperament both as a person and a writer, and a conscious understanding of your expertise and where your interests lie, you can improve on your luck considerably.

Get Passionate

In one way or another, all the stories of successful nonfiction writers looked at here speak to the same thing: a passionate involvement in writing. That's the key to success, either personally or monetarily. Given the highly competitive market of freelance writing, few writers are so good they can slack off and not give 100 percent of themselves on every piece. And writers cannot give their best unless they're downright passionate about what they're doing. Few people in any endeavor can. The only difference in writing, as compared to selling insurance, for instance, is that in writing a bad attitude is conspicuous; it shows in the writing.

The underlying presumption in a passion for writing is, in a very real sense, a passion for life. How else are you going to find something worthwhile to say and then say it with conviction?

"Never embark on a project unless you are deeply fascinated by it," writes contemporary journalism's unparalleled muckraker, Jessica Mitford, in *Poison Penmanship: The Gentle Art of Muckraking.*

I went into journalism because I saw it as a way to be a perpetual student. I could learn a lot of interesting stuff and get paid for it. It's more or less worked out that way. As a newspaper reporter, I soon learned that I had to learn a lot of boring stuff—try sitting through a city council's mosquito abatement hearings—which is one reason I switched to freelancing. Now I spend more time pursuing what interests me. There's little job security in it, but it's worth it.

So, first thing, become mentally engaged in the world. An innate curiosity helps a lot. Emotional engagement also helps, if you want writing that is more than lifeless. Since you've come this far in your pursuit of nonfiction writing, you are probably engaged in the world to some extent already. But if not, seriously question your decision to write. If you decide to carry on, then decide what ignites your intellectual and emotional passions.

In an ideal world, you'd only write about what ignites your passions. But we all live in the real world, regardless of our varying degrees of denial. Which means you must decide how much you are willing to compromise, if at all, about the kind of writing you pursue. Which gets back to what kind of person you are. Are you practical? Uncompromising? Stubborn? A dreamer?

Along with your psychotherapist and spiritual advisor, writing can help you decide.

CHAPTER TWO

Where and How to Get Nonfiction Ideas

Everything has been thought of before, but the problem is to think of it again.—Goethe

About the most originality that any writer can hope to achieve honestly is to steal with good judgment.—Josh Billings

M any novice writers look to the creative writing talent they know they possess as their ticket to the top. According to their scenario for success, their fancy literary footwork will wow them in editorial offices all over the country, not to mention the other thirty-odd countries where their work will be translated.

While talent, meaning in this instance writing style, is unarguably important to success in article writing, it is arguably not the key element. Perseverance and self-discipline are also not to be underestimated. But in the long run ideas are paramount. At the risk of stating the obvious, every piece of nonfiction is an idea, actually a collection of ideas, made manifest in writing. Without ideas, you have nothing on which to lavish your bedazzling style. Many successful nonfiction writers may point to their unique styles as what differentiates them from their competitors—and it is undoubtedly true—but probe a little deeper and you'll find that behind the styles lie fresh ideas, or more likely fresh ways of looking at old ideas.

Within the first week of my joining a daily newspaper—my first—
my editor sat me down for a chat. She wanted to get a few things
straight, namely what she expected from me. "Not everyone has great
style," she said, "but style isn't most important. Ideas are. I pay you
for ideas." Thereafter, I was a man on a mission. I searched relentlessly
for ideas, because my editor relentlessly demanded them.

But don't take my word for it, or the word of some city editor. Let's
have Tom Wolfe, the man who put creative nonfiction, once known
as New Journalism, on the literary map, weigh in on the subject.

"That damnable beast, material, keeps getting bigger and more ob-
noxious," wrote Wolfe in his 1990 essay for *Harper's*, "Stalking the
Billion-Footed Beast." "You realize you have a choice. Either hide
from it, wish it away or wrestle with it. I doubt that there is a writer
over forty who does not realize in his heart of hearts that literary ge-
nius, in prose, consists of proportions more on the order of 65 percent
material and 35 percent talent." Wolfe was addressing himself to writing fiction, but certainly his words apply to nonfiction as well.

So, now that we all understand just how important ideas are to
nonfiction, where do story ideas come from? The short and not altogether flip answer is, everywhere. Story ideas come from the sum of
your life experience. They come from everything you read, from the
movies and television programs you watch, from the plays and concerts you attend, from discussions with friends, family, acquaintances
and colleagues, from chance encounters with strangers, from your observations of others in daily life, from the problems, challenges, quirks
and joys in your own daily life. It's an embarrassment of riches out
there.

The real problem is how to sort through the mass of information
and sensory stimuli that assault you daily to find good story ideas—
while at the same time maintaining your curiosity and continuing to
look at the world through fresh eyes and with a sense of wonder.

Write What You Know

"Write what you know" is usually the command given out to novice
fiction writers so their writing rings true. But that same command
slightly revised, can apply to nonfiction writers as well. Some stories
lie so close to home that you can trip over them and still fail to

recognize them as grist for the mill.

I know a writer who knew a story when it literally stared him in the face. He saw it every morning when he looked in the mirror. He noticed—he couldn't help but notice—that his forehead was growing larger as the years progressed. To put it bluntly, he was going bald. This fact inspired an idea for a lighthearted article about male-pattern baldness using himself and his father, who is also bald (part of the story—baldness is in the genes), as subjects. He sold the story to *Health* magazine, and that story was in turn picked up by *Reader's Digest*. (He also wrote a variation of it for a few alternative weekly newspapers.)

I once got news about a former colleague thanks to his perceptiveness about how events in his own life reflected a larger social phenomenon. His byline was attached to a story about how single men who reach their forties are more often than not presumed to have psychological or emotional problems, to account for why they're not married. This is quite a change from years past, his article contended, when a bachelor was often seen as independent, distinguished or dashing. As you might have already guessed, this former colleague had been a confirmed bachelor. He did not use himself in the story, however; he interviewed other confirmed bachelors. I saw his story in my local newspaper, distributed through the Los Angeles Times Syndicate.

Another writer I know built a new wing on her career at the same time that she was raising two young sons. She wrote articles about child-rearing, now her specialty.

Look at your own life. What about it is common to the experience of millions? Are there aspects that have not been explored or for which there is a continuing, compelling public interest? Look at your own hobbies and other recreational interests. Do you like to garden, play tennis, collect antiques, fly fish? Your occupation, if you have one other than writing, can also prove a rich source of ideas. Plus, you have the built-in credibility to call yourself an expert. A writer-photographer I know who supports himself primarily as a physician has authored a book on terminally ill patients who were considering suicide. He has also written articles for magazines and newspapers on subjects in which he brings his medical expertise to bear.

And when you're looking for ideas, don't forget your personal relationships. There's a large market out there for articles on human interactions and essays that wax philosophic on the vagaries of life from a first-person point of view.

In the course of doing whatever it is you do, be it work, play or in your personal relationships, all kinds of problems and rewards will present themselves. If you're thinking critically, you'll see how they might serve as nonfiction ideas. In short, and to put it bluntly, cannibalize your life. That's what it's there for.

Know What You Write

While you don't want to overlook the nonfiction ideas that center on your own immediate interests, you need to venture outside those interests if you want to maintain a well-supplied stock of good story ideas. In fact, many beginning nonfiction writers commonly, and lazily, look around and choose to write about the first thing that captures their attention. Experienced writers can also fall into the same trap, also from laziness, but often they've become jaded and have lost their interest or passion in exploring the world around them.

One of the reasons I got into journalism was precisely to get outside of myself, to lose, and loose, myself in that big world beyond. I wanted to belong to something larger than myself. This is a motivation for many other writers as well, and perhaps you, too. Venturing out into the world intellectually and emotionally, and then physically, is ultimately essential for personal satisfaction as well as an abundant supply of nonfiction ideas.

Learning about what you don't know and then writing about it is akin to continuing your education on a scholarship. As far as I'm concerned, that's one of the best things about being a nonfiction writer. People pay you to learn about stuff, and all you have to do in return is write a little report about it.

When I decided that I wanted to learn about how to buy a house, I went out and got a job with a real estate financing newsletter. The company paid me for my education in real estate, and I turned that knowledge into a successful, real-life version of Monopoly. When I bought my first house, I knew more about financing than my agent; I explained aspects of financing to him. It was a wonderful feeling, since most first-time home buyers feel like helpless children and look to their agent as a hand-holding parent. I subsequently did another, fairly sophisticated transaction, the kind in which few residential lenders or agents ever get involved. And I owe it all to an education I received at someone else's expense. Is that a sweet deal, or what?

Pick an area to specialize in that interests you, then simply study the subject. Get a few articles published, in low-paying publications if need be, and suddenly you're an expert. Gregg Levoy, a former newspaper reporter, decided that science and health were fertile fields to cultivate as a freelance writer. So he studied those subjects, sold a few articles, and . . . presto! He became a specialist. One assignment then led to another.

So, the axiom "write what you know" still applies but, with a twist: Know what you write. You can greatly expand the quantity and quality of your story ideas by learning enough about a subject to write adeptly about it. This involves work, namely research, but that's your job as a nonfiction writer. First, you research to get ideas, then, with assignment in hand, you research those ideas to get finished articles.

Scissors Cut Paper

When I first got started as a newspaper reporter, standard issue included, among various and sundry things, a pair of scissors. The scissors were to be used to cut up as many newspapers as I could get my hands on, at the very least mine and the competitors'. Many of the other stationery accoutrements I received—paste, tape, stapler, paper clips—were to aid me in achieving that end. I cut and filed articles that gave me ideas for stories.

I read the newspapers first thing in the morning, standing up. If you looked across the newsroom, you'd see many other reporters reading newspapers also while standing. By standing, we could look through the paper quicker. But there was more to it. The body language said a lot. By standing, we were not relaxed. We were tense, ready, alert. We were on a hunt. We were searching for story ideas. I still read the morning papers (note that's *papers*, plural) with a pair of scissors by my side. I do sit while reading, but only because it's hard to chew toast while standing hunched over a table.

I share this little anecdote by way of saying that to find ideas for articles you need to develop an attitude—an attitude of analytical detachment. The goal of most fiction and much nonfiction, feature articles certainly, is to cast a spell upon you the reader, to transport you from your mundane world into that other, more exciting world that the writer creates. That's also the goal of movies, plays and many television programs. You must resist the storyteller's magic, because if you fall under its spell then you won't be able to discern its elements; you'll simply be bedazzled.

A professional nonfiction writer, and arguably a fiction writer as well, is a professional observer. This holds true not only when you're reporting in the field, which seems obvious, but also when you consume information, whether in a deliberate search for story ideas or when reading, watching or listening for pleasure. Unfortunately, the truth is there really is no such thing as reading, watching or listening for pleasure once you've committed yourself to writing. The search for ideas—in a larger sense, the search for meaning—is never ending.

Don't, by the way, confuse analytical detachment or professional observation with being objective, an attribute sometimes still extolled in newspaper reporting but now mostly set aside in favor of fairness. You can, and probably should in most cases, take a point of view in your nonfiction writing. But still you need this sense of analytical detachment to not let story ideas slip by unnoticed.

It takes little effort to see that perpetual observation is a curse. It can interfere with your personal life, as many a writer has discovered when every act, every intimate encounter, instantly turns into raw material. The writer and monologuist, Spalding Gray, who gained notoriety with his movie, *Swimming to Cambodia*, commented upon this phenomenon in his book, *Gray's Anatomy*.

" 'Great Spirit, please don't let me turn this experience into material for another monologue,' " Gray quotes himself as he writes about the time he participated in a sweat lodge ceremony in hopes of curing an eye problem through spiritual awakening. The Great Spirit was not smiling upon poor Mr. Gray that day. In thinking that thought, Gray foretold his fate.

Fortunately for Gray, perpetual observation hasn't blunted his enthusiasm. But it can render you, and thus your writing, jaded. So you have to know when and how to use this lens or filter of analytical detachment, and when to leave yourself open to the magic of the world around you. Somehow, Gray has managed to do both.

With print material, you can read like a civilian and then go back and examine it critically, or bypass the pleasure reading and go right to the critical examination. In real life, when you're out in the field observing and interviewing, you have to assume one attitude or the other, depending on what the story calls for, or, difficult but not impossible to do, assume both at once.

The Media Pyramid

It is often said, snidely and cynically, by professional journalists that by the time a trend makes the cover of *Time* magazine it's over. *Time* is a ponderous media beast. It has the burden of speaking to (and for, as *Time* apparently sees it) the entire nation, and more specifically, middle America. So a trend has to be well established, which often means after it's peaked, before *Time* will give it official sanction. By the time *Time* featured Generation X, the label for the post baby-boom generation, on its cover, the man who had coined the term and was considered its chief spokesperson, novelist Douglas Coupland, had renounced the Gen X phenomenon. Consider this for lag time: The Generation X discussion group on the computer conferencing system known as The WELL began *two years* before *Time* published its cover story.

Trends grow from the grassroots, in other words from the bottom up. News about trends and developments in the arts, science or whatever, unless it's breaking, hard news that major news organizations will obviously report, likewise percolates from the bottom up. That is, the information appears in more specialized, less widely distributed publications and forums before reaching the major news organizations or prestige publications. The exceptions are articles that raise questions about topical issues that others don't, or raise important issues that no one else has thought to raise, or take a fresh look at a subject, old or new, in a way that enlightens the reader. It is in large part precisely these kinds of stories that have made magazines such as *The New Yorker* and *Atlantic Monthly* prestigious.

At the top of the print media pyramid are the *Time*s and *The New York Times*es of the world. In the middle are the metropolitan newspapers and leading consumer magazines in broad market categories such as fashion, travel and health. Farther down the pyramid are local newspapers, academic journals and the smaller circulation consumer and trade magazines, often with increasing specialization—*Snack World*, a magazine for food vending-machine operators, comes to mind. Then there are the fanzines, also known as zines, the computer desktop published magazines that often reflect the skewed perspectives and concerns of their very small-time publishers. At the bottom are the vast array of industry and organizational publications, newsletters, news releases and other propaganda, as well as the staggering tonnage of local, state and federal governmental reports and publications.

Add books, and you've just accounted for print. Television and radio have their own hierarchies. And now there's the newest wrinkle in information exchange, the estimated twenty million people who communicate via computer networks, and all of the print material that is now available electronically.

Climb the Media Pyramid—Up, Down and Sideways

Obviously, you can't cast your information-gathering net over the entire media mass, not if you want to actually write anything, not to mention eating and sleeping and walking the dog. As discussed in the previous chapter, you have to focus on your chosen area or areas of specialization. The trick is to travel up, down and across the media pyramid picking up information, getting ideas and doing research, and then depositing it somewhere else in the form of articles you write and sell. This can involve stealing ideas outright—you can patent ideas but you can't copyright them—and selling them nearly intact or slightly repackaged to another market. More often, however, the information you discover will inspire your own ideas. You'll then write and place articles either in the same market, or in another market as differentiated by geography, demographics or topic. You'll usually get more and better ideas the lower down the pyramid you travel, because as stated above, the stuff closer to the bottom is closer to the source.

Get Connected

In almost any area of human endeavor there's a network of people talking to each other, usually through a variety of media. You need to go beyond your own magazine subscription list and frequent trips to the library or newsstand to monitor newspapers and magazines. That's only part of the picture. You need to get plugged in—fully.

Join organizations or get on their mailing lists. This is the way to wade hip deep in their full flow of networking information. They'll send you newsletters, brochures, flyers and special missives on issues of major concern. You'll receive announcements of conventions, seminars, luncheons, mixers and the like, and you'd be a fool not to attend some of them to talk to people and observe firsthand what's going on.

Get on public relations mailing lists. It's estimated that more than one-third of what you read in the newspaper is instigated by public relations people. Whatever the percentage, public relations (also known as public affairs, media relations and community relations— they can't seem to settle on a single term) represents an important source of information. You don't have to swallow all the propaganda P.R. people want to force-feed you; pick and choose according to your own agenda.

The Information Superhighway you've heard so much about is huge, and it's here to stay. Learn how to use it (a whole chapter later in this book will get you started). You can chat electronically with people interested in a particular subject via online bulletin boards, and tap into publicly available databases that pertain to your interests.

One of the most important ways to stay plugged in is to cultivate personal contacts, in other words, to develop sources. Get on the phone and talk to people in the field, including people in government and people in the private and nonprofit sectors. Better yet, if you have the time and it's important enough, go see them in person, to develop a personal rapport.

If you feel uncomfortable approaching strangers and asking for their time and expertise, remember it's your job as a purveyor of nonfiction to extract information from knowledgeable sources. In other words, you have license to pry in your role as a journalist. Besides, most people are flattered to be solicited for their opinions; few people care what they think most of the time. And, of course, you'll be polite and appreciative.

Don't let too much time lapse between contacts with sources. You don't have to be working on a story to call them. In fact, it's a good idea to touch base with your sources when you're not working on a story. Just ask how things are going, or broach a broad subject area you'd like to learn more about. Your sources are likely to mention something that might spark an idea for a story. Sources are as much or more sources for story ideas than for expert information on specific stories.

Cultivate your sources at various levels. People at the top of a business, organization or government agency usually have the best handle on policy, as well as the big picture of their organization and field of interest. But they're usually out of touch with what's happening on the ground. Middle managers and others who live in the belly of the organizational beast—and even lower, in the bowels—make the best sources when you want to know what's really going on at ground zero. They're also much more willing to talk candidly, albeit often on background, than official spokespersons and those at the top, whose job it is to put their best spin on a situation. People in the middle make excellent sources, being not too far from top or bottom. They're often knowledgeable about policy, the machinations of organizational bigwigs and what's happening on the ground. Organizational foot soldiers will tell you stuff that has not yet percolated up the chain of command.

By cultivating sources and regularly monitoring the written communications of organizations that focus on a particular issue, one thing will lead to another and soon you'll find that you, too, are an insider. You will become part of the network, rather than the casually interested journalist who drops in for information on a subject from time to time. This way, you'll learn what's about to make big news, and you'll develop the contacts and depth of knowledge to find well-focused story angles and to write the "inside" story. And that is what editors want, especially from freelance writers. In short, you'll become an expert, a major selling point to editors.

File and Forget Me Not

You will undoubtedly become so proficient at generating story ideas that a creative avalanche will soon overwhelm you. You'll forget all the wonderful ideas you thought up earlier as you think up some more. You're just going to have to write them down. Think of each new idea as a project; open a file on it. That's where those newspaper and magazine stories you've been clipping belong, along with the notes you make when talking with sources, the brochures and news releases you get from public relations people, the reports you get from organizations and governmental agencies, and the random thoughts and ideas you jot down when you think of a story or see an article that triggers an idea.

This last habit, writing down odd thoughts, is immensely important but often overlooked. Inspiration is a wonderful thing. Make it work for you. From time to time, great ideas and small but important details related to developing a particular story idea pop into your head; it's your subconscious cogitating on an idea. Perhaps you're waiting in line at the bank or stuck in traffic or washing the dishes. Write it down as soon as possible, or you're apt to forget it, and then stick those scraps of paper in the proper file.

By the way, note the source and date of every scrap of paper you keep. Forgetting to do so will prove nettlesome when you refer to them months or years later. Also, highlight key words or phrases in the documents you file so you remember why you filed them in the first place. Highlighting makes your job easier and quicker when you review your files. You might also want to attach notes to clippings and other documents to put the information in context and to record related thoughts.

It's probably not practical to start a file for every new idea, a goodly number of which will not pan out once you've done some preliminary research. But you can keep files on broad subject areas you intend to pursue, in addition to specific stories.

For my travel writing, I open a file for each country I'm planning to visit. Depending on how many articles I subsequently write and how much backup information I accumulate, I keep all the material in the country file grouped by story or I might also start adjacent files on specific stories. For example, I opened a file on contemporary Thai artists, which was for a story I wrote for Delta's in-flight magazine, in addition to the general file I had already opened on Thailand.

I also keep a catch-all, miscellaneous ideas file for stories within the U.S. that are more culture or human-interest oriented than strictly travel stories. In addition, I keep more general files divided by continent, in which I file articles I clip, odd scraps of information and notes on story ideas that I might get around to when hell freezes over.

Many nonfiction writers also keep a "futures" file of stories they need to check on or write by a certain date. Since, I confess, I sometimes file ideas and then forget about them (out of sight, out of mind), I note on my calendar dates when I need to act on a story.

The Customer's Always Right

Your job as a nonfiction writer is to engage the reader intellectually and, more often than not, emotionally. Therefore, a writer's first and most unbreakable rule, the prime directive as it were, is *make it interesting*. This would seem obvious, but you'd be surprised how many people, writers included, overlook the obvious.

Oftentimes, writers are so preoccupied getting the details of a story—the facts and story organization—straight, they forget they must also entertain the reader. And these days, with all the competition from other media for a person's time and interest, and the inherent advantage of sensory stimuli that movies and television have over print, articles must be more than interesting, they must be compelling or downright exciting. They must grab the reader by the throat from the very beginning and never let go.

Who Is the Customer?

Before you can give the customers, that is the readers, what they want, you have to know who the customers are. If you set as your goal breaking into the top women's magazines, for instance, it helps to know the reader demographics of those magazines. OK, they're women, right? Well, yes, as far as it goes. But there are a lot of women out there, and adhering to the law of self-interest, they choose their magazines in relatively neat demographic clumps (or rather, publishers market their magazines to neat demographic clumps, all the better to serve up those clumps to advertisers). So, *Redbook* readers are women twenty-five to forty-four years old with children twelve years of age or younger, and almost two-thirds of them work outside the home. *Cosmopolitan* readers, meanwhile, are eighteen- to thirty-five-year-old working women. As you can see, there may be some overlap, but different magazines emphasize different concerns of even overlapping readership. In *Redbook*, for example, the slant is on children and family life, as you would expect from the reader profile. *Cosmo* tilts heavily to concerns outside the home, i.e., the workplace, and romantic relationships most often of the nonconnubial kind.

It's easy to tell who a magazine's customers are. *Writer's Market*, published by Writer's Digest Books, sits on most nonfiction writers' reference shelves; it supplies a wealth of basic information about magazines, including reader demographics. For more detailed information, you can write for a copy of a publication's writer's guidelines before submitting an article proposal. And of course you should *study the magazine*. Studying the magazine can't be emphasized enough. Study the articles not only to see what kind of information they deliver but also in what form they deliver it and in what style and tone.

Also study the advertisements. In some ways, the advertisements give you a more accurate reader profile than the editorial content. Advertising usually deals with readers' realities—advertisers can't sell what the reader can't afford—while appealing to readers' dreams, desires and insecurities. Editorial content, on the other hand, may appeal to readers' aspirations and to fantasies that readers may never attain. The average reader of women's fashion and beauty magazines, for instance, can scarcely afford the *haute couture* these magazines sometimes feature. If you still can't figure out who exactly reads a certain publication, phone the publication and ask. The first person who answers the telephone in either editorial, marketing or ad sales can probably tell you what you want to know. If not, ask to speak to someone who can, but it's best not to bother a senior or associate editor with such questions.

If you decide to write for markets rather than first finding the stories that inherently interest you (in reality you'll probably do a bit of both), you must know your markets so that you know what you're looking for when you search for ideas.

What Does the Customer Want?

So, what makes a story interesting? Compelling? Exciting? First and foremost, the human element, whether comedy or drama, because all stories are ultimately connected with people. Even more to the point, however, what makes a story interesting, in all cases, boils down to one, hyphenated word: self-interest. Whether it's an article appealing to an abstract but enlightened self-interest that believes what benefits society benefits the individual ("Improving the Nation's Educational System") or the more obvious, self-centered self-interest piece ("Six Easy Ways to Tighter Abs") it's still self-interest.

In the interest of self-interest, the reader has but one question when starting to read your story: What's in it for me? Upon reading your story proposal, the editor will ask the same question on behalf of the reader. So you'd better ask that question, too, when you're thinking about story ideas.

Catering to the more parochial reader self-interest is particularly true now that the magazine industry is fragmented into narrow marketing segments—all the better for publishers to deliver potential consumers to advertisers. A market segment refers to readers typically of a similar sex, age, income, marital status and of similar interests, which a magazine hopes to attract with its editorial content (articles). Magazines may focus on an overall lifestyle, as do *Playboy* and *Cosmopolitan*, but more often they focus on a subject, say, golf or food. As magazines fragment into narrower categories to reach a more focused market for advertisers, you see magazines such as *Cooking Light*, which is about low-fat cooking, and *Meals in Minutes*, for chefs on the go.

Articles in most consumer magazines often emphasize positive stories, or perhaps disturbing stories with positive or optimistic outcomes, although stories that outrage readers or push other emotional hot buttons also have currency. Rarely do they challenge their readers to examine preconceived notions. You can take it upon yourself to push the edge of the journalistic envelope and pitch stories that appeal to enlightened self-interest. There is still a place in magazine journalism for these kinds of stories. But a writer with an established reputation or who has developed a relationship with a magazine probably stands a better chance of successfully pitching stories that a magazine ordinarily eschews than a writer trying to break into a market.

For newspapers, the dictum to always give readers exactly what they want as opposed to what writers and editors think is good for them is less true. Newspapers are much less segment-market driven than magazines, although readership is slightly older, and newspapers' mission historically has been to serve as a forum for public debate about the issues of the day. With increasing competition from other media for people's attention and the attendant decline in newspaper circulation, however, newspapers have also started to give readers more of what they want. That often means lighter articles and articles that confirm rather than challenge readers' preconceptions, and less of what editors think readers need to be well-informed citizens.

Cheap and Easy Idea-Generating Techniques: A Checklist

Fortunately or unfortunately, your nonfiction, and especially a magazine article, is as much a product as is beer, a car or perfume. Here are a few tried-and-true things to look for when searching for story ideas:

Superlatives. People love superlatives: the first, last, oldest, youngest, biggest, smallest, fastest, slowest, highest, deepest, tallest, shortest, best, worst and only. Those are the usual suspects, but any others you can think of will do, too. Editors love superlatives because people love superlatives. Don't ask me why. Maybe because it gives them something concrete to focus on. In any case, superlatives delight people no end.

Some articles are entirely about superlatives. An article in *Backpacker*, for example, titled "Giants of the Earth," lists places to visit the largest animals, whales, the largest trees, giant sequoias, and even the largest fungus, which the article claims is located in Washington state and may be the largest living thing on earth.

Some superlatives are themselves topics of enduring interest. Take the highest place on earth, Mount Everest. In 1994 and 1995, Mount Everest spawned a *Forbes* story on the increase in tourist treks to the mountain's base, stories about a trash cleanup effort by American mountaineers showed up in *Audubon* and *Sports Illustrated*, and a story about the mountaineers who attempted to reach the top during one month, May 1994, appeared in *Maclean's*.

What's New. Same as the "first," except the subject has just become the first or will become the first in the near future. Hence the word "news." And as any advertising person will tell you, the word "new" is one of the most attractive words of all, perhaps second only to "free." In print, newspapers tend to have the inside track on what's new. When Neil Armstrong walked on the moon, no one waited around for *Time* to report it. But what's new may not be so obvious or earthshaking. A writer with an insider's knowledge in a given field can get to market first with a first.

Take the example of a *New York Times* profile in "The Living Arts" section about a Miss Teen-Age America finalist. Early in the piece, writer Jennifer Steinhauer informs us that "for the first time since Miss Teen-Age America's inception, thirty-three years ago, there will be no appearance category." Steinhauer then offers up her profile subject, Heather Hegedus, as an example of a new breed of pageant contestant, one in which brains and character are emphasized over physical appearance. The article is aptly titled, "Miss Teen-Ager as Queen of Smarts."

What's new most often falls into the province of fast-moving media such as newspapers, radio and television. But a profile of Heather

Hegedus could have also worked paradoxically for a fashion and beauty magazine aimed at teenage girls.

Trends. An acute observer puts together pieces floating around the cultural ozone and concludes that a new social phenomenon is under-way—it's a trend. A trend is bigger and more important than a single event. It is a new development in a field such as business, science or the arts, or a new social phenomenon in which an increasing number of people are involved. A trend builds over time, which is especially important to magazines, thanks to their long lead times compared to newspapers, which are more likely to report on individual events. More important than long lead times, however, is that magazines are trend-mongers because almost by definition their purpose is to inform readers about subjects within the context of contemporary times. A trend is the nonfiction writer's gold.

Spotting a trend comes directly from research. It's a matter of having your ear to the ground, otherwise known as talking to sources, and constantly reading both general interest and speciality publications. To differentiate a genuine trend from media hype, find studies and reports indicating whether a phenomenon is increasing with significant numbers of people or whether it is really only confined to a small and static group.

An article published in *The New York Times Magazine* in February 1995, for example, reported that contemporary Christian music, also known as CCM or white gospel, was then the fastest growing form of popular music. Christian pop music had been around for several years, so the phenomenon itself wasn't new in 1995, and numerous articles about Christian pop music had already been published. But writer Nicholas Dawidoff claimed that Christian pop had reached "critical mass" in only the previous few years, amounting to upwards of $1 billion a year in sales. In effect, the "critical mass" description of CCM signaled the writer's assertion that CCM now constituted a bona fide trend, not a mere fad, which is a degraded or ersatz trend more suitable for movie-fan rags than the Sunday magazine of the nation's most prestigious newspaper.

Some might argue, however, that the *Times* was a bit behind the trend curve on this one, which is why the news peg was couched in terms of "critical mass." But the precise time a fad becomes a trend is an editorial judgment call. The article mainly described the CCM phenomenon. It profiled top CCM artists and CCM fans through interviews and descriptions of concerts.

A less ambitious but perhaps more viscerally satisfying trend story (for the writer, anyway) was the short piece that appeared in the December 1993 *Esquire* about the country's increase in beef consumption. The article duly noted the increase with a single statistic, and offered a few reasons such as the beef industry's $42 million ad campaign and the urge to splurge in economically tough times. That all took one paragraph, the opening paragraph. For the rest of the story, writer John Berendt repaired to a New York restaurant to consume a slab of the world's most expensive beef, a Kobe steak, at $100 a slice. Tough assignment.

Challenging Conventional Wisdom. Although magazines most often publish articles that reinforce their readers' beliefs, sometimes they like to liven things up by challenging readers' prevailing views. Writers who question conventional wisdom can find print space with a well-reasoned argument. Arguments backed by statistical evidence and other facts are even better.

The *Atlantic Monthly*, generally considered a liberal publication, specializes in part in challenging conventional wisdom, be that wisdom liberal or conservative. When former Vice President Dan Quayle, for instance, criticized television sit-com character Murphy Brown for giving birth to a baby out of wedlock, the news media played up the incident as another of the vice president's wacky outbursts: Quayle was doing battle with a fictional character as if she were real. Most news organizations confined themselves to reporting Quayle's comments and the avalanche of ridicule that followed. But months later the *Atlantic*, no friend of the conservative Quayle, published Barbara Whitehead's cover story, "Dan Quayle Was Right," which explored the issue of fatherless families and concluded that such arrangements harmed children and eroded society.

Another *Atlantic* article, titled "The Sex-Bias Myth in Medicine," also questioned liberal beliefs, this time the widely held belief that medical research is biased toward men and against women, and that medical practitioners treat men's complaints more seriously than women's. The logical extension of those beliefs suggests that men receive more and better medical treatment than women. Writer Andrew G. Kadar amasses statistics and studies to argue the opposite.

And once again wading into the quicksand of conventional beliefs, the magazine published "Reefer Madness," which showed that despite widespread belief that marijuana use has been *de facto* decriminalized, about one-sixth of federal inmates are doing time for marijuana offenses, and sentences meted out for marijuana crimes are often harsher than those for violent crimes, including murder. The 1995 National Magazine Award for reporting went to the *Atlantic* for its reporting on law enforcement of marijuana.

Former Trends, aka History. Some magazines, such as *American Heritage*, are devoted to former trends, while others, such as *Smithsonian*, are historically minded in that they publish one or two historical features in every issue. But many other magazines publish histories as well, often as a means to advocate for current issues or to explain the historical context in which current issues are being played out. In its November-December 1994 issue, *Modern Maturity* did all of the above. Under the heading, "The New Civil Rights," the magazine featured an article about the history of the disability rights movement. Interspersed alongside the main story are four shorter articles, or sidebars, about current aspects of disability rights. While the main article is basically a piece of reportage, the sidebars take advocacy positions. The subject is an apt one for *Modern Maturity*'s readers; even most able-bodied people become disabled in one way or another as they grow elderly.

Personal Essays. Personal essays, including memoirs, have grown into a large genre of nonfiction writing. As journalism becomes more personality driven—the rise of *People* magazine testifies to the phenomenon—readers crave intimacies that encourage writers to turn themselves into subjects. Magazines such as *Details* publish sections in every issue consisting of first-person pieces, while others, such as *Smithsonian*, often devote a column or the last page to a personal essay from a non-staff contributor. Many newspapers also set aside standing columns for freelance, first-person contributions. The *Christian Science Monitor* has one entitled "Home Forum," where I published an article in which I inserted myself as a character to tell the story of a World War

II veteran. Several years ago *The New York Times Magazine* instituted weekly alternating "Hers" and "About Men" columns. The *Times'* Sunday travel section also publishes first-person essays every week on its penultimate page.

Personal essays are often inspirational, and almost always pack an emotional punch. Such essays are a staple of *Reader's Digest*. One such article condensed from the *Berkshire Eagle* told how a mother coped with her son's growing up and leaving home. Another, from *Guideposts*, told how a mother's bequest of a desk to her adult daughter signaled the mother's approval of her daughter's chosen career.

Anniversaries. Anniversaries are, in a sense, another "first," but all over again. They are perhaps the most important way we maintain our collective memory. They also give editors a chance to publish articles they otherwise wouldn't. Round numbers work best, those ending with zero or five, and especially ten, twenty-five, fifty, seventy-five, one hundred, etc. Oftentimes the story angle is simply the anniversary itself.

Look at all the stories pegged to the fiftieth anniversary of significant events related to World War II: the bombing of Pearl Harbor, D day, the liberation of Auschwitz, the bombing of Dresden, the Battle of Iwo Jima, the atomic bombings of Hiroshima and Nagasaki, and of course the German and Japanese surrenders. And they weren't just newspaper stories marking the events themselves. Magazine articles took innumerable approaches. In *Travel Holiday*, for example, a writer accompanied a former Auschwitz inmate, now an American, back to the Auschwitz concentration camp for a ceremony recalling a failed uprising in which her sister was shot and she was almost killed. That ceremony obviously predated the fiftieth-anniversary commemoration, but the article was timed to appear for the fiftieth anniversary.

Seasonal Events. Seasonal events articles are similar to significant anniversary years but better; they're newsworthy every year. *Martha Stewart Living* and other magazines devoted to hospitality and homemaking provide fertile ground for planting seasonal stories. An issue of *Bon Appetit* ran a section titled, "Food for April," which consisted of three articles on foods and cooking most suitable for spring. Various magazines also regularly publish travel articles timed to help readers with their summer vacation plans. *New Age Journal* published an article about how one can turn a vacation into a pilgrimage even though the magazine infrequently covers travel. An article about the desert bloom appeared in the "The Living Arts" section of *The New York Times* on the first day of spring. The article explained that heavy winter rains and warm weather had produced an especially abundant bloom that year. And another *Times* feature detailed the travails and hopes of actors during the New York theater community's annual mass auditions, otherwise known as cattle calls, which take place in spring.

Self-Improvement. Americans' greatest obsession is perhaps themselves. They want to improve themselves mentally, emotionally and physically. They want to improve their financial situation and personal relationships. As a people traditionally optimistic, they want to have it all. And magazines, eager to hold and expand their market segments, enthusiastically show the willing reader the way. In fact, self-improvement articles, also known as service pieces, have become the dominant genre in magazines. They come in many forms and guises. There are "how to" articles, "how not to" articles, instructional articles, and articles about problems the reader may encounter and strategies for dealing with them.

Some magazines have virtually given themselves over to self-improvement. Take *McCall's*, specifically the March 1995 issue. Of eight articles promoted on the cover, and therefore signaled as the issue's most important stories, six are related to self-improvement in one way or another. They include "Nine Ways to Fight Deadly Infections," "How Not to Be Fired" and "Old-Fashioned Ways to Raise Kids." In fact, almost every article in the magazine deals with some form of self-improvement. A few others are "The World's Easiest Workout," "Three Hidden Causes of Fatigue," "Deadly New Infections You Can't Ignore" and "How to Get a Brand-New Butt."

Self-improvement can also take place on the more sublime level of enlightened self-interest. An article in the *Atlantic Monthly* titled "Moral Credibility and Crime" argues that the rules and procedures in the criminal justice system have eroded the system's own moral authority. Writer Paul H. Robinson further argues that social science research suggests that social approval, in other words, peer pressure, is the most potent factor in governing human behavior. Robinson then proffers ten steps to inject moral authority into the criminal justice system and thus put the system right.

Perennial Favorites: Subjects for Any Story

It seems that readers can't get enough of some subjects. And while writers may understandably have no wish to wallow in sex and celebrities, they ignore, at their peril, how these subjects can spice up their story ideas. The "sexier" a story is, the more likely you are to sell it.

Body Basics. Nothing so excites us, as a nation, as our physical urges and bodily functions. As you know, the areas of sex, food and health are so vast that whole market segments are devoted exclusively to them. And as you also may know, articles about basic urges pervade most major market segments. Major topics of conversation in the women's magazines, and many of the men's magazines (that are not already devoted exclusively to sex), consist of food and health, and sex in its broadest meaning, from intimacy to romance to down-and-dirty lust. Even the one other big topic, clothes, is strongly connected to sex, and to food and health as they pertain to improving status or sex appeal. The examples here are so numerous they're overwhelming. Stop by the magazine rack at your local supermarket to see the latest crop on display.

Celebrities. Even more than sex, maybe, celebrities sell. (You've probably noticed how celebrities and sexiness are all mixed up together. Celebrities are often celebrities because they're sexy, or their celebrity status adds an aura of sexiness to them.) Famous people have always been the subject of public curiosity, of course, but in the past generation or so the public appetite for celebrity has seemed insatiable, resulting in a corpulent body politic, many a social critic would contend. Nonetheless, if you want to sell articles it helps considerably to write about celebrities or to work celebrities into your story. Not everyone can bag an interview with Madonna, but big-name celebrities, not to mention second-, third- and fourth-rate celebrities, will lend their names and give a few quotes for a good cause, say the prevention of child or animal abuse.

Even the august *New York Times Magazine* has been known to use celebrity to juice up a timely but not necessarily exciting subject. The magazine ran an interview with Michael Milken, he of insider-trading, junk-bond infamy, entitled, "Michael Milken Fights a Hostile Take-over." The story was about Milken's prostate cancer and his attempts to find a state-of-the art cure. At the time, a spate of prostate cancer stories were appearing in the nation's news media.

Colorful/Notable Personalities. This is a subset of celebrities. These are people with fascinating lives, and preferably amusing, quirky or dynamic personalities as well. They may be celebrities to a particular group or locale but little-known to the wider public. They're local heroes, or maybe they just do quirky things that brings them notoriety, or perhaps they're infamous.

A *Playboy* piece, titled "Death of a Deceiver," by Eric Konigsberg, tells the story of Teena Brandon, a young woman who masqueraded as a man and whose secret sexual identity was revealed publicly only upon her murder. If you lived outside of Nebraska, where the story took place, perhaps you read a small item in the newspaper about the strange circumstances of her life and death, as I had in the *San Francisco Chronicle.* So, Konigsberg sets out to tell you the story behind the story of this minor, regional celebrity, whose celebrity was earned by the unconventional behavior her murder brought to light.

Mix and Match

Celebrity anniversaries, new celebrities, celebrities by virtue of being the oldest, only or first. Celebrities and self-improvement. Celebrities and sex. Sex and self-improvement. The variations are endless.

In the previous example from the March 1995 *McCall's,* two of the cover-promoted stories mixed celebrities with self-improvement: "Joan Lunden's A.M. Beauty Secrets" and "How Whoopi [Goldberg] Got It All." The *Playboy* article about male impersonator Teena Brandon is about sex and minor celebrity. An *Esquire* article titled "Sex and Prozac" is a sex and health and trend article. It explores whether the "drug of the nineties," as the subhead describes Prozac, retards the sex drive of its devotees. I once received an assignment from the California Division of Tourism to write about the fortieth anniversary of the death of movie star James Dean for its quarterly tourism magazine. The story combines celebrity and anniversary, and since it involves a dead celebrity, history, too. But the best in show has to be the *Cosmo* theme issue of April 1995: "Sex in Hollywood."

On a less frivolous note, an article in *Modern Maturity* entitled "Take Charge of Your Pain" is ostensibly a health and self-improvement piece. But it is also a trend piece, as the brief article description in the table of contents hints: "One of our most common health problems is shamefully undertreated. But you don't have to suffer." While it is true that the medical profession has historically undertreated patients' pain, the profession itself has actively addressed the problem recently through what it calls pain management. The article really uses this trend in medicine as the springboard for self-improvement, that is, to reshape the reader's conception of pain. As the medical experts in the article argue, doctors underprescribe pain medication because many patients strongly resist pain relieving drugs. Patients believe taking drugs, even to relieve pain, to be immoral or are afraid they will become addicted. They also believe that bearing pain is admirable. Writer Mary Batten quotes a medical expert to state the theme of her article: " 'Pain is more than a passive symptom of disease. Pain is an aggressive disease in itself that needs to be controlled as soon as possible.' "

So it seems that many surefire, salable ideas load up on as many idea devices and popular issues as possible. Which leads the conscientious article writer to ask: How many hot buttons can tango in 2,000 words or less?

Putting the Pieces Together: A Case History

I once planned a trip to Tucson, Arizona, to visit a friend. Since in the past several years I've focused on travel writing, in an attempt to remain a generalist under the guise of a speciality, the first thing I did was contact the local visitor's and convention bureau for the big package of promotional material I was sure they had. They sent it to me—it was a *hefty* package—and I quickly noticed an "only" that piqued my interest: the Titan II Missile Museum, the only underground nuclear missile complex open to the public.

An instrument of mass destruction is a highly negative subject to say the least and an abstract concept to boot, as opposed to the more personalized destruction of street crime. It is a hard sell, except maybe to the *Soldier of Fortune*, war-is-glamorous market, a market I'll be content never to break into. But with the collapse of the Soviet Union, an underground nuclear missile complex struck me as a relic of the Cold War. It was history, but it was also news, since the Cold War had recently ended—it was new history. I queried history magazines, and not so coincidentally, the editors of *American Heritage* were planning a major article on the Cold War nuclear buildup for a companion quarterly called *Invention & Technology*. My article on the Titan II Missile Museum fit nicely with the featured piece.

Without having wide-ranging interests that encompassed current events, I probably would not have thought to place a missile complex in the perspective of recent history. (The nation's nuclear arsenal is of course still operative, but its importance has diminished in the face of greatly diminished adversaries.)

The story also appealed to my personal interests. I had been involved with the nuclear weapons freeze movement prior to the end of the Cold War. That involvement also yielded a well-placed story. At a convention, I learned about a network television miniseries that many people considered inflammatory to Soviet-American relations—several months before it aired. My inside knowledge of what I believed would become a news event, an event in which Hollywood and celebrities figured, positioned me to place my story prior to the event but timed for publication with the show's broadcast. I sold an op/ed piece to the *Washington Post* criticizing the miniseries as classic political propaganda. I identified myself to the *Post* editors as a chapter president of a well-known, citizen organization concerned with nuclear issues and American-Soviet relations. I suspect this tag of authority, or expertise, helped sell the article, though the piece also had to sell based on its merits.

The trick to finding story ideas that are both personally satisfying and salable is to mesh your skills, expertise and interests with magazines' needs, which focus on discrete market segments. You must also stay attuned to trends and developments important to readers so you can offer magazines cutting-edge stories.

CHAPTER THREE

Shaping and Refining Ideas

*I am a camera with its shutter open, quite passive, recording,
not thinking.*—Christopher Isherwood

Mirrors should reflect a little before throwing back images.—Jean Cocteau

All too often, beginning nonfiction writers produce articles that read like term papers. They'll decide to write about the homeless, for example, a worthy topic, and then proceed to tell readers everything they ever wanted to know about the homeless and then some in a logically constructed report beginning at *A* and ending at *Z*. After reading the piece, a reader is moved to ask, "What was the point?" The report turns out to be the kind of thing you'd literally have to pay someone to read, in other words, a teacher. Most everyone else would quickly become bored and move on to more interesting and entertaining reading. Which is what they should do. Settling on "the homeless" as the subject of an article reveals a stunning lack of imagination by the writer.

Imagine instead the following scenario:

The seasoned journalist asks, as an editor would ask if confronted with such a proposal, "What about the homeless?"

The Neophyte: "Well, they're poor."

The Editor: "Great. Now tell me something I don't already know."

"Many of them are mentally ill or are drug or alcohol addicts, or both."

"Terrific. That would have been interesting when we first started seeing homeless people on America's streets and didn't know much about them. But since then there have been plenty of stories about who they are, their mental illnesses and addictions. When are you going to tell me something I don't already know? Are there more homeless now than there were ten years ago? Are there less? If there are changes, why? Are the demographics of the homeless changing? Is there recent legislation or public policy that has affected their lives?

"We know about the homeless mostly from official sources, but what's it like to actually live as a homeless person? Why don't you spend the next two weeks living as a homeless person—no going home at night for a hot shower and a warm bed? What's it like, and how well does the system work, or not work, in taking care of homeless people? What are the irritations, inconveniences, indignities and deprivations that homeless people suffer daily?" (Notice how important research is to this approach, but more about research in succeeding chapters. To accomplish this little-done story, the writer is going to have to leave the comfort of home or the office and get out into the street, and possibly some physically and emotionally uncomfortable situations, to get this story.)

"By the way, are they all poor?"

"Well, actually, no. A few are castaways from wealthy families."

"Hmm . . . that's interesting. A new wrinkle. A bit quirky. Let's do it. Let's tell their stories, who they are and how they got to be where they are. It's a new twist on an old line. The rich are different than you and I—they're living on the streets in shabby clothes. OK, perhaps it is a somewhat marginal, some might even say frivolous, aspect of a serious subject, but inquiring minds want to know."

Perhaps a story about rich homeless people is a bit far-fetched. But who knows? It might serve as a cautionary tale for readers of *Town & Country*. From time to time, even rich people long to stray off the farm, horse farm, that is.

Less ridiculous yet no less arcane articles about homelessness published in the early 1990s included "Serving the Homeless Through Recreation Programs" in *Parks & Recreation*; "They Found $2,394 . . . And Gave It Back" in *Family Circle*; and "What a Formerly Homeless Man Learned in the Public Library" in the *Education Digest*.

Weightier articles about the homeless have dealt with medical treatment of homeless people, evolving public policy and reasons to account for the increase in homelessness.

An article in *Researcher* explored a debate about whether individuals or government and private charities can more effectively deal with homelessness. On one side are people who see large organizations as cumbersome, inefficient and insensitive to the needs of the homeless. Those on the other side argue that community spirit is too weak to adequately sustain individual and organized grassroots efforts. The debate, and thus the article, arose from the simple, basic question: How can we best solve the homeless problem?

An article in *Nation's Cities Weekly* reported that low-income renters had increased since the eighties while low-income housing had declined. The article argued for a realignment of federal housing aid. And an editorial in the *New England Journal of Medicine* called for adequate primary care for disadvantaged people as part of any governmental, comprehensive health-care reform. The editorial used research information gathered from a health-care program for children living in welfare hotels and homeless shelters. The research indicates that inadequate health care accounts for much of homeless children's poor health.

As you can see, the more serious articles about homelessness were published in specialty magazines by and large, not mainstream consumer magazines. This tells you something about the current public interest in homelessness, which is to say, not much, except as approached from an obtuse angle. So, if you want to write about homelessness, you must make certain decisions about the kind of article you want to write and the marketability of that article.

The examples of homeless stories listed above, and more examples listed below, suggest that successfully marketed articles focus on an aspect, or angle, of a topic, and the more focused it is, the better.

Angle for Ideas

Beginning newspaper and magazine writers write about topics: Professionals look for angles.

One topic can beget a thousand questions. And out of a thousand questions comes the focus, or angle, for an article.

Sometimes, a topic itself is newsworthy, but usually because it is new; the subject's newness is the angle. The big article on homelessness made sense in the 1980s, when large numbers of homeless people started appearing on city streets nationwide. Quickly, however, writers looked for various aspects of homelessness to write about, and even when the phenomenon was new the topic was really too large to do it justice in a single article.

Out of a trip to Spain, I received assignments from two airline in-flight magazines. One was on sherry; the other, on Madrid. Before leaving on the trip, I had queried the editors with some general ideas, which included sherry as a Spanish invention and Madrid's famously active nightlife. It took only some preliminary research—reading over guidebooks, newspaper and magazine articles and looking over the tourist office's propaganda—to come up with these general ideas.

Once I ventured into the field, however, I found a sharper focus for each story. It turns out that what constitutes genuine sherry is little-understood outside of Spain, and Madrid's nightlife reflects one facet of Spain's national character.

I pitched sherry to United's *Hemispheres*, which has a regular department on wine and spirits, and Madrid to Delta's *SKY Magazine*, which regularly runs features on cities along its routes. The editors themselves did not initially have specific ideas. The editor at *Hemispheres* liked the idea of a story on sherry and Spain because it gave the magazine a chance to cover both areas in one article, in effect, to kill two birds with one stone. And all the editor at *SKY* knew initially was that she needed a story on Madrid because Madrid was on her list of cities for that year.

The editors were interested in my story ideas, but they withheld giving me a definite assignment until after I had returned and pitched them the more sharply focused ideas, which I'm sure made my pitch more appealing. Just like anyone buying anything, editors feel more comfortable knowing exactly what they're going to spend their money on before they spend it. Given other circumstances, editors may assign stories based on vague ideas, how well they know the writer being an important factor, but in general the sharper the focus the more compelling the pitch and, ultimately, the better the story.

In one sense, a story angle is like a shell game. It's really the same story but told from a different . . . well, angle. You've heard the old saw: There's nothing new under the sun. But what's important is whether the angle hooks readers and keeps them interested.

In many cases, the truth works something like this: I say—and indeed the editor says, though we don't often say it to each other—I want to do a story about Madrid, or some other subject. Then I find a way of writing about Madrid that hasn't been done (too much) already. Madrid as the city that never sleeps (along with New York) is done every so often, but national newspapers and magazines weren't saturated with the story when I proposed it. Plus, I put extra spin on the story by positing that Madrid nightlife is an expression of Spanish character.

My angle for sherry was to disabuse readers of their notions and introduce them to the genuine article. Referring back to the "Cheap and Easy Idea-Generating Techniques" of the previous chapter, you'll see that my idea fit the category of trend contrariness, and because I presumed most readers knew little about sherry, it was something new.

While, as in the examples above, editors may often need angles as excuses to cover topics, at other times they may only look for the interesting or unusual take on a story, with the subject being secondary. In either case, ultimately you must find a sharply focused angle for your story.

An angle not only casts even an old and tired subject in a new and fresh light to capture readers' attention, it also helps readers organize and shape a story in their own minds. When I read a story I want to know fairly quickly what the story is about, that is, what the angle is. I need the writer to lead me along, to give me a context in which I can understand the story.

National Geographic, for example, tends to take a big picture approach to its articles, especially articles about destinations, a city, region or country. The approach is a sweeping, detached, on-high view (though more intimate approaches have been allowed in recent years). But despite the on-high perspective, the articles still give readers something to hang on to.

In the opening paragraphs of an article about New Orleans, senior writer Priit Vesilind sets up New Orleans as a city with a traditional image of a mythic lush life—the image that gave New Orleans the nickname the Big Easy—contrasted with problems that have beset the city in recent years. Then he writes the following one-sentence paragraph: "I came here to see if New Orleans had held on to its soul." The article, then, is an investigation into this issue. Has New Orleans changed, and if so, how? Is it still the same Big Easy that has made it unique among American cities? Readers now understand the context in which they will read about New Orleans.

Every good story has such a sentence and such a paragraph, the one in which the writer plainly tells you what the story is about. It is usually fairly high up in the article, as part of the opening, and it even has a name. It is commonly called the "nut" paragraph.

Finding a story angle is easy. Just keep badgering yourself with questions. The traditional five *W*s of journalism work well—who, what, where, when and why—along with the *H*, how. What about Madrid? What about Madrid nightlife? Why Madrid nightlife? How Madrid nightlife? Where Madrid nightlife? Who? When? In this case, it's the "why" that gives the story character; Madrid's robust nightlife reflects the *joie de vivre* of the Spanish people, or as some Spaniards told me (during a week of delightful field research), "Americans live to work but Spaniards work to live."

Angle for Markets

In the many articles written about homelessness, writers matched aspects of homelessness with publications that might have some conceivable affinity with those aspects. So, for instance, an article in *Essence*, a beauty and glamor magazine targeted at African-American women, consisted of an interview with the 1994 Miss America, an African-American of course, about her work on behalf of homeless people. An article in *House Beautiful* reported on a benefit auction of refurbished chairs that raised $15,000 to help needy families. And an article in *Advertising Age* reported on an innovative program in Las Vegas by which homeless people advertise their availability for work via public service announcements on television.

One method to determine a story's various marketing angles is to write a one-sentence synopsis and then divide the sentence into its key components. This works especially well when you're writing about a person or group of people engaged in an activity. The Miss America story, for example, would also work for a general women's magazine, and a newspaper or regional magazine covering the geographic area where the program she works with is located. The Las Vegas public service announcements article would also work for local Las Vegas publications, and there's also probably a publication covering the religion, ethnicity or professional or service association of the person who thought up the PSA idea.

Weave a Theoretical Thread

Whereas an angle is a piece of a topic looked at in a certain way, the theme is the theoretical thread that holds the piece together. To take the example of my article on Madrid for Delta, the angle was this: Madrid's remarkably active nightlife. The theme: Spaniards possess a *joie de vivre* that is amply exemplified in Madrid's nightlife.

After a two-paragraph opening in which I described the busy scene in Madrid's central square at midnight, I wrote the "nut" paragraph, which included the sentence informing the reader what the story was going to be about: "The myth, sustained by a healthy dose of reality, persists that Madrid is a city most awake at night—all night."

And in the fourth paragraph, I imply the theme rather than state it explicitly, to be more artful, I hoped: "Spaniards like to say, politely yet with a whiff of superiority, that Americans live to work, but Spaniards work to live. So for this American reared on Puritan values ('Early to bed, early to rise. . . . '—thanks, Ben), coming to terms with Madrid's *joie de vivre* was not easy, especially when so much of it took place well past my bedtime."

The theme informed nearly every fact I included in the article, and my interpretation of those facts. For instance, in describing the scene at a tapas bar, I emphasized Spaniards' penchant for socializing: "Patrons packed the place and were wreaking convivial havoc upon it, as well as themselves, with a blizzard of eating and drinking and loud talking. The din was truly impressive. Barely keeping up with the barrage of orders, the bartender furiously worked the beer-tap handle while an assistant slapped little plates of tapas on the bar. . . ."

I carried this aspect of the theme further in the succeeding few paragraphs. First I related a bit of cultural dissonance. I wrote that my American companions and I complained to our Spanish hosts that we were spending too much time on meals. We thought of meals as pit stops, not as a cultural activity. "But we failed to understand," I wrote, "that eating and drinking are secondary concerns. The main course at any Spanish meal is conversation."

That provided the segue for me to explain the Madrid institution known as *la tertulia*, a regular gathering of friends or colleagues for discussions, similar to a salon.

I also described how Madrid still reverberates from *La Movida*, The Movement, the cultural and sexual freedom that erupted in Spain following Franco's death in 1975. I constructed my ending, a scene of an elegantly dressed couple coming out of Madrid's legendary, *belle epoque* Palace Hotel near dawn, to support my theme.

The theme came to me vaguely in the course of field research. It filtered up through the mass of information I was gathering as I looked for patterns to connect the various bits of information. The theme clicked for me consciously when, in reflection, I recalled the Spaniards who had told me, "Americans live to work, but Spaniards work to live." This line rang true to me, as I judged from my travels in Spain, and not just Madrid.

The important point is that I knew my angle and theme before sitting down to write. That made it much easier to organize the facts I wanted to use in the story and to write with a point of view. If you can think through your piece before you write, all the better. It is true, however, that sometimes you can only discover your theme, what your story is about, in the writing of your piece. It's also true that it then means more work, that your writing had been by and large an exercise in discovery. You then must often do more rewriting than would otherwise be the case, so the unifying theme of your piece clearly emerges in the written work, unless subconsciously you'd already woven it in.

One Story, One Idea

Angles and themes work hand and hand. Unless you want to make a mess of your articles, allot only one idea to each story; save the many-faceted subject for your book. Take a point of view on that angle, and then make every sentence drive home your point. In fiction, it's the difference between a novel and a short story.

The following sections explain how to focus, or shape, stories further to make them cohesive, coherent and manageable. Essentially, these are exercises in delineation: Generally, you want to exclude much and include little. You can delineate the information you use or don't use by applying certain story-shaping techniques to the material itself, such as adjusting the scope of a story according to story length or approaching the material either microscopically or macroscopically. But you can also delineate through ways of perceiving the story, such as point of view and tone. They also place boundaries on the story, firmly guiding readers through the information you present, rather than letting them wander bewildered in a maze of ideas, concepts and facts.

Function Follows Form, and Vice Versa

Determine what form you want your article to take—is it a service piece or a narrative?—and to a large extent you've shaped your idea. You could very well find that your idea doesn't fit the form you've selected, so you select another form. And then find another idea to fit the form you've just abandoned.

Let's go back to the topic of breast cancer to see how this works. Say you want to write about the latest techniques for breast self-examination. You could write a profile on the medical professionals who developed the new techniques, but that wouldn't make a lot of sense if you're trying to educate women about those new techniques. A how-to, service format would work better, perhaps with a list under the title, "Six New Ways to Prevent Breast Cancer." In such an article, you would briefly mention the individual or institution responsible for the new techniques and then move on to the techniques themselves. Save the profile for the professional or trade journal, in which you'd expand on the personalities and briefly outline the techniques.

You could write about the pros and cons of radical mastectomy versus lumpectomy in a question-and-answer interview with a noted authority who tries to give readers a balanced evaluation, or perhaps with an advocate of one side, if you want to present only one side. You might also try a debate format, with an expert advocate on each side responding to the same question. You could also write a narrative of a case history, or a few case histories, and show their outcomes.

Scope out the Situation: A Story's Scope

Gone, by and large, are the days of the 5,000-word feature article for magazines like *Collier's* and the old *Saturday Evening Post*. You'll still find long articles in a handful of magazines such the *Atlantic Monthly* and *Harper's*. But with people having more media from which to choose for entertainment and shorter attention spans thanks to television, magazine articles have shrunk to attract readers. Even the *New Yorker* has cut to size its famous 10,000-word articles in an effort to attract younger readers. About the only market wide open to writers who want to stretch out and write long pieces, and try out fiction techniques in nonfiction writing, are in what are commonly called alternative newspapers: the primarily local, tabloid-format, weekly newspapers that mainly cover arts, entertainment and, to a greater or lesser degree depending on the paper, local politics. Now the vast majority of magazines typically run articles ranging from 1,000 to 1,500 words for department pieces, and 1,200 to 2,500 words or maybe 3,000 words for features.

So when it comes to nonfiction articles, you have a fairly small canvas on which to work. Don't try to paint an epic scene. You won't be able to get all the important elements in, and if you try, they'll be too small or lack the details to make a proper impact. Trying to paint a miniature on a larger canvas can also be a problem, but this is not a problem most writers face. It's almost always a case of trying to shoehorn too much into too little space. Joan Didion once said she writes long, involved sentences as a way to save space.

The best way to cut your article to fit your editor's word count is to cut your story, that is, confine the scope of your story to the allotted space. The shorter the space, the narrower the focus. You take a small piece of a topic or larger story and explore it fully within the confines of your space. Scope, then, is a way to define the boundaries of your story subject.

Let's take two examples from business writing, one of which works well, and the other, not quite as well.

An article in *Fortune*, titled "The Risks Are Rising in China," mostly focuses on intellectual theft in China. The lead paragraph states that the widespread, illegal duplication and sale of American movies, pop music and computer software by Chinese companies is "the latest evidence of the growing and increasingly visible risks confronting Western and Asian companies doing business in the People's Republic."

The lead appears to contain the nut paragraph. But, then, so does the second paragraph. The second paragraph lists as old news a few of the other risks—inflation, corruption, political instability and fickle government policies—and that China's potential to become the world's largest market within a generation outweighs the risks. The paragraph's last sentence reads: "What could well slow the flow of that investment are the prominence of the companies running into trouble, the size of their potential losses, and the growing awareness of just how deeply rooted China's problems are."

It appears the story is now about how large companies are beginning to rethink their investment strategies in China in light of their problems there and their potential losses. And indeed, the third paragraph provides evidence, namely McDonald's real estate leasing problems, Lehman Brothers' lending problems with state corporations, and a foreign banking consortium's lending problems.

But the fourth paragraph switches back to pirated copyrights and stays there for the rest of the article, which is a department piece of approximately 1,500 words. The article explains the hows and whys of intellectual piracy in China and what the United States is doing to stop it. Big companies are named as the victims of intellectual piracy, but nowhere does the writer support the qualified contention that the problems of doing business in China "could well slow the flow of that investment."

It seems as though subject drift set in during the second and third paragraphs. The article's title and subhead reflect the story's wavering focus in the initial few paragraphs. The subhead reads, "Take an ailing patriarch, inflation, rampant corruption, and a culture that considers counterfeiting cool, and what have you got? A pile of potential problems." It's as though the headline writers read only the first four or five paragraphs and figured they knew what the story was about.

In fact, this story could have been about how companies are rethinking their investment strategies in China in response to the problems of doing business there. That certainly would have broadened the scope of the story.

The *Fortune* article also deals only briefly with possible solutions to intellectual piracy in China. Two paragraphs toward the end of the piece summarize the news event that appears to have triggered the timing for this and other stories on intellectual piracy: U.S. retaliation through increased trade tariffs and China's own retaliatory tariffs. In addition, the article's last two paragraphs point to the Taiwan experience as a possible solution. Product counterfeiting and intellectual piracy decreased when Taiwan developed intellectual property of its own worth protecting.

A longer, more in-depth story would delve deeper into these areas, using detailed examples to show step by step how Taiwan's attitude toward intellectual theft changed, and perhaps examining how well punitive trade barriers worked in similar situations to get countries to change their policies. Did the U.S. or other countries use tariffs against Taiwan? Analysis from experts on how likely it is that tariffs will work against China would also help the reader to better judge the situation and how soon, if at all, the situation will change.

A story in *Forbes* about Allstate's decline and recovery is more focused throughout than the *Fortune* piece, and that's reflected in the title and subhead. The piece is entitled, " 'We Grew Too Fast,' " and the subhead reads, "Allstate Insurance caught market-share fever. After a painful bout and a painful cure, it's healthy again."

The story delivers exactly as advertised. Writer Marcia Berss mentions external factors hurting Allstate such as hurricanes, rising interest rates and unfriendly regulators, but then she focuses on the problem of Allstate's own making. She explains that, in a fit of market-share fever, Allstate relaxed underwriting standards and hired more agents. But the company couldn't generate enough profits to build the reserves legally required to fund the expanded sales volume. To right itself, the company cut back, improving its profit performance. Berss also discusses Allstate's plans for furthering its turnaround, such as developing a sales force of independent agents.

This, too, is a relatively short department piece. A feature story might have fully explored Berss's lead sentence: "Insurance stocks are under a cloud." Such a story would flesh out how rising interest rates and unfriendly regulators hurt the industry as a whole, why some companies were hurt more than others and what strategies various companies are using to get themselves into sunnier weather and how well those strategies are working. As it is, Berss immediately signals to readers that she is going to deal with only one company. Her second sentence: "Allstate Corp. is no exception."

Get Ahead of the Curve: The Mature Story Versus the Juvenile

The aforementioned homeless example points to the different stages a subject evolves to in the public consciousness and therefore public discourse. Sometimes story angles just get more exotic or arcane, or they can chart a social phenomenon's permutations and more deeply explore its implications.

The subject of breast cancer has received an enormous amount of coverage in recent years, yet the market for breast cancer stories is by no means exhausted. An InfoTrac search showed scores of entries for breast cancer articles in magazines from 1992 to 1995; care and treatment alone, one of forty-three subcategories, listed sixty-eight articles. Like the subject of the homeless, breast cancer has spawned some narrowly focused, arcane articles such as "Cabbage Cuts Cancer Risk" in *Organic Gardening* and "Good Day, Sunshine" (on the health benefits of sun exposure) in the Sierra Club magazine, *Sierra*.

But breast cancer is a more dynamic subject than the homeless for a variety of reasons. Breast cancer potentially affects many more people than the likelihood of homelessness, and the public demand for solutions accelerates scientific research and public policy decisions, to name two. In that light, new wrinkles and trends in breast cancer prevention and treatment provide a steady stream of articles to mainstream publications.

A *Redbook* piece entitled "Desperate Measures" was about women undergoing preventive mastectomies; an article in *Science* entitled "Restating the Risks of Tamoxifen" related how a drug to treat breast cancer might carry additional risk of endometrial cancer; and *New Republic* questioned the effectiveness of mammography public policy in a cover story titled "How Safe are Your Breasts?"

Even with single-event stories, as opposed to unfolding stories or subjects, such as breast cancer and homelessness, you can find stories by looking deeper than the obvious surface events. You ask questions that get to the core of a story, and do the research required to answer those questions.

That's what editors and writers at *The New York Times* did in part to win a Pulitzer Prize for national reporting on the *Challenger* space shuttle explosion. One article in the series that won, by Stuart Diamond, looked beyond the immediate facts of the explosion to examine systemic problems in the National Aeronautics and Space Administration. Diamond reviewed more than five hundred federal audits of NASA, many of which were obtained under the Freedom of Information Act. He found that budget problems in NASA induced administrators to cut or delay half a billion dollars in safety testing, design and development while at the same time these same administrators ignored inspectors' warnings that they were wasting huge amounts of money through mismanagement. He buttressed his documented findings with interviews with space experts both inside and outside government.

Examine With Your Microscope, Macroscope: Story Approaches

When it comes to a big story, say one which is multidimensional or has numerous elements, nonfiction writers face a daunting task. How to approach it? How to get a handle on it? How to make it as concrete and understandable to readers as possible?

There are a few basic ways to go about it. You either pick one example and explore it in detail, or, like some god from Olympus, you take an overview, shaping your story according to the conceptual elements that make your point.

The Microscopic Approach

In the first approach, you basically put your example under a microscope. You examine it minutely, and show the reader how the various issues involved in your story work on your subject, subject here meaning the person, group of people or company or institution you are using as your example.

The strengths of this approach are that you in effect provide readers a concrete case study, which often is an easier way to understand a complex subject. Harvard Business School, for example, uses the case study approach to teach students about business concepts. When you've given your story a human face, as it were, your topic becomes more real for readers and your story, with its often built-in narrative line providing a beginning, middle and end, becomes more compelling.

The drawbacks are that the argument for the case you're making, if indeed you are trying to persuade the reader to your position on an issue, may appear less authoritative and thus less convincing precisely because you are providing anecdotal evidence. Even if you include a paragraph or two high up in the story, as such stories often do, containing statistics to demonstrate that your example is a fair representation of an issue or that the problem is big enough for the reader to pay attention to, your story remains anecdotal. A microscopic approach also, by definition, makes it harder for readers to grasp the big picture. And, lastly, what if you decide to take the microscopic approach and then can't find an interesting enough example? So first make sure that whoever or whatever you choose for top billing in your story is a star.

The Macroscopic Approach

The macroscopic approach essentially flip-flops the pros and cons of the microscopic approach. The macro approach is more abstract, and thus harder for readers to grasp readily, but it can make a more authoritative, convincing case to readers. By its nature, it allows them to see the big picture, but they get few of the myriad details that allow them to understand the story in as much depth as they might with a microscopic approach. And it lets you select the cream of the crop when it comes to anecdotes to illustrate your points.

The Combined Approach

A middle way can also work. It has the dramatic, human element and also the convincing argument that the phenomenon is widespread, a true trend, rather than being specific to an individual or small group. More important, it lets you pick the most dramatic anecdotes to illustrate your points. The downside to this middle way is the same downside as most middle ways: It's neither here nor there. You can end up with less weak weaknesses but no real strengths. The story might simply become mush.

Weighing the Pros and Cons

An article in *Smithsonian* about a solo, round-the-world yacht race provides a good example of the micro-macro choice a writer must make when covering a story. The race involves twenty competitors from seven countries and lasts several months. The writer, Wendy Mitman Clarke, chose to focus on an American competitor, Steve Pettengill, which made sense since she was writing for an American publication. She organized the piece in diary form, by date and time; fifteen entries ranging from November 22 to January 3. This structure recalls a captain's logbook, putting the reader in a nautical frame of mind.

By taking the micro, personal approach, Clarke's story focused on what life is like for one competitor in a highly challenging race rather than the race itself. She delved into myriad details, from the meticulous preparations Pettengill made to sail around the world solo to the various conditions with which he had to cope, to bring to life for the reader a sense of what it is actually like to be in such a race. She creates such a complete picture of Pettengill and his yachting endeavor that the reader can identify with him personally. The personal connection compels the reader to continue reading. A macro approach, or big picture view, of the race could never yield such a personal portrait. There simply isn't enough space even in the relatively longer *Smithsonian* articles, which average about 4,000 words, to provide a comprehensive portrait of several competitors. The wider focus also necessarily forces the writer, and reader, to take a more detached view of any one competitor.

But Clarke's close study of an individual competitor must necessarily sacrifice the advantages of the macro approach. Clarke had to forgo the built-in conflict, and thus drama, of a race, as well as the easy, logical narrative structure a race invites—beginning the story at the starting line and ending at the finish line. The story also becomes more descriptive than active, and thus less compelling. Clarke is describing Pettengill's life on the water, despite the logbook conceit, which suggests movement, rather than reporting the race and its inherent suspense.

Clarke also had to forgo choosing the absolutely best, most dramatic, most harrowing, most compelling stories from among the competitors because she was pretty much locked into following Pettengill. She does hedge her bets, however. In one entry, she reports that Pettengill finishes second in the first leg of the race. This gives her a chance to mention the only woman in the race, a French engineer named Isabelle Autissier; Autissier finished first. Then to work in a good story about another racer, as well as demonstrate the unexpected pitfalls the racers face, Clarke writes the following segue: "Autissier wants to be the first woman to win it [the entire race]; Pettengill wants to be the first American to do the same. They know, as does every racer, anything can happen." She goes on to tell about a racer whose boat hits something hard in the middle of the Atlantic and how he desperately bails water for nine hours before another competitor rescues him. Because her article is about Pettengill, however, Clarke must tell this story in an abbreviated fashion.

Clarke's tack here suggests a middle approach that can sometimes work: choosing a few individuals, a small group or a locale and its people as the microcosm with which to illustrate a larger issue. Clarke's micro approach made more sense for *Smithsonian* than a macro approach would have. *Smithsonian* is a magazine about science, art and culture, ultimately about how people live in the world, how we affect the world and the world affects us. So the life of a yacht racer is enlightening and entertaining to *Smithsonian* readers, and it is a subject presumably few readers know about in great detail. Such a story would probably be too general and basic, and thus not too interesting, to readers of yachting magazines. They might be more interested in an article about how the current BOC Challenge racers are trying to gain the competitive advantage, say in boat design.

A big factor in Clarke's, and *Smithsonian*'s, decision to go micro was undoubtedly timing. The article appeared one month before the race was to end, which made the article timely and generated extra interest in the race. Clarke could not have covered the race without writing about the big finish—talk about denying the reader a sense of closure. An article about the previous year's race also would not work. Most sporting events are evanescent by their nature. Except for a few memorable games, and more typically memorable moments rather than whole games, sporting events are strictly present-tense affairs. Once the game is over and the winner is known, the suspense disappears instantly; the interest quickly wans. The reader would have little emotional investment in the fortunes of last year's competitors in relation to this year's race.

Clarke had to decide whether to go micro or macro before the serious, intensive, information gathering phase of the story began. Even if she could seemingly be in two places at once, closely covering an individual and the entire field, she would have made an immense amount of extra work for herself. Either approach requires a considerable amount of research for a magazine article.

The decision about micro versus macro can significantly affect how strongly you make your case on issues more important than yacht races, especially if the issues are fraught with controversy, like sexual harassment in the workplace, for instance. A macro analysis appeals to the intellect; the micro case study more often than not goes for the emotions.

An *Esquire* article, titled "The Joke That Killed," tells the story of a man who committed suicide after an accusation of sexual harassment against him resulted in the company, AT&T, suspending him and then transferring him to the corporate equivalent of Siberia. The article contends that the company essentially acted based only on the accusation, without any supporting evidence. This seems to be the article's point: In responding to sexual harassment in the workplace, companies have gone overboard.

Writer Christopher Byron briefly sketches the broader issue fairly early in the piece. He lists a few of the better known sexual harassment cases, such as Anita Hill's accusation against Supreme Court Justice Clarence Thomas and Paula Jones's accusation against President Bill Clinton, along with a few of the more absurd examples of the lengths to which institutions have gone in their attempt to provide a harassment-free workplace (a fifty-year old Works Progress Administration mural in Illinois that depicted Indians in loincloths was covered up in response to a postal employee complaint).

"Thus, it has become more difficult to draw lines, and the response of people in authority to questions of sexual harassment has often been unthinkingly automatic," Bryon writes.

Interestingly, however, he provides no statistics to demonstrate the breadth of the problem as he sees it. We see no statistics on the number of sexual harassment cases filed in the past few years or how they've been resolved as compared to previous years. Perhaps no such statistics exist; the writer should say so if that's the case.

He offers instead anecdotes and conceptual argument: The definition of sexual harassment has broadened to the point that now "according to the courts and the Equal Employment Opportunity Commission, the law basically leaves it up to the complainant to say whether he or she has been offended by the conduct in question."

Perhaps Bryon takes the micro approach, the extended anecdote, because while some companies may have unjustly punished workers accused of sexual harassment, the numbers of these cases may be few. Considering what it appears he has to work with, Byron has taken the most effective approach; an incident with emotional impact that provokes outrage in readers, *Esquire* readers at least, who are mostly men.

Make Connections, Think Ahead: Ramifications

Time and events rush on, and newspaper and television news reporters throw themselves into the breach every day to get the story. As a freelance nonfiction writer, you can take a more relaxed, deeper approach to events thanks to the news minions on the frontline of history. You can ask: What does it mean to those involved? How will it affect their lives? In the short run? In the long run? What are the ramifications?

Jacques Leslic, who was mentioned in the first chapter, has carved a magazine niche for himself based on ramifications, writing as he does about the social and cultural impacts of computer technology.

This approach enabled Leslie to write "Mail Bonding" for *Wired*, an article about e-mail twenty-five years after it began. Having by then some historical perspective, Leslie examined how e-mail has affected communication between individuals and within institutions, and as it relates to politics. He offered as an example a business success story in which a multinational corporation dramatically improved communications within its far-flung sales force by using e-mail.

In his story, Leslie pointed to his own example as limited: "The only trouble with success stories like these is that while they demonstrate the power of e-mail, they do nothing to illuminate its complex impact on corporate climates, and therefore they may be slightly misleading."

Leslie was preparing the reader to delve deeper into e-mail's ramifications. He explained that researchers call a technology's anticipated changes, such as improved communications, "first-level effects." They refer to unanticipated changes as "second-level effects," and this is where the game gets really fun. He cited two researchers who found in one study that men were five times as likely as women to propose first a decision in a face-to-face meeting of business executives but the ratio evened out when the meeting was held via computer. Another study found that e-mail inhibited managers from candidly discussing personnel matters and politically sensitive issues because e-mail leaves a record.

You can look ahead as well as backward. You can extrapolate to look at possible future ramifications. What, if any, chain reactions will occur? You can anticipate them and write about what's likely to occur in the future.

Freelance writer Douglas Fine sold a Sunday feature article to *The Washington Post* about how ensuring the preservation of mountain gorillas in Rwanda could help rebuild that country following its bloody civil war. Fine pointed out that the gorillas drew Western tourists, and Rwandans needed the hard currency the tourists brought to rebuild their devastated country.

Get Physical: Action Versus Analysis

Conflict is just as inherently dramatic in nonfiction as it is in fiction. In conflict is suspense and action. The article moves, and moves inexorably to a climax, simply by virtue of the story's circumstances. There are heroes and villains, or maybe, in neat little twists, heroes and heroes facing bad circumstances, or a pair of villains engaged in metaphorical mud wrestling, or most intriguing, a little of hero and villain in each of the main characters.

Players, that is people who act in and upon a situation, are more compelling to read about than observers who comment upon the action or experts who analyze a situation. A plethora of hard facts is perhaps worst of all; the eyes glaze over at an article filled with numbers. Even in articles without narrative lines, it's better to concentrate mainly on those involved in the action rather than analysts, although analysts can provide authoritative, objective commentary on the action, and observers can supply a different, and presumably enlightening, perspective. So it's a good idea to add a comment here and there from an observer or analyst to frame the action, give it context, or to add veracity and depth. Just don't make your story top-heavy with observation and analysis and light on action, unless, of course, the point of the article is to analyze an issue.

An article in *Playboy* titled "The Guru and the Gadfly" tells the story of how the falling-out between New Age guru John-Roger and best-selling author Peter McWilliams affected the outcome of the 1994 senatorial race in California. In short, Roger Delano Hinkins had a vision, changed his name to John-Roger, built himself a New Age empire, acquired among his many devotees successful writer and publisher Peter McWilliams and Arianna Stassinopoulos Huffington, wife of California Congressman, soon-to-be senatorial candidate, Michael Huffington. John-Roger had a falling-out with McWilliams over royalties on a book the two wrote and McWilliams published, not to mention McWilliams's denouncing of John-Roger as a phony, whereupon McWilliams mounted a publicity campaign to discredit John-Roger, and as a part of that campaign tied Arianna Huffington to John-Roger, whereupon the media ran with the story, further besmirching Huffington's already questionable reputation.

In addition to the built-in conflict and narrative line of how John-Roger and McWilliams came together and then fell apart, this article has several things going for it. First, it involves celebrities. The two main characters in the piece are minor celebrities in their own spheres, while the candidate caught up in their dispute, Michael Huffington, and Huffington's wife, Arianna, are known to the public at large. The race garnered much national media interest, mainly for two reasons: Huffington spent twenty-nine million dollars of his own money on the campaign, and then after losing by a razor-thin margin, he refused to concede defeat until months later.

Arianna Huffington's connection to John-Roger also piqued the media's attention in the campaign. And, according to writer Bob Sipchen, Peter McWilliams was the man who put the media onto the Huffington/John-Roger connection as part of his vendetta against John-Roger. So, Sipchen's tale, subtitled "The Strange Adventures of a Best-Selling Writer, a New Age Spiritualist and a Very Rich Congressman," is one of those perennial favorites, the story behind the story, the inside story, the kind of story that invites readers to feel they belong to an elite group by virtue of possessing inside information.

In the article's opening scene, John-Roger, McWilliams and a group of reporters are in the parking lot of "Hollywood municipal court." (Just hearing "Hollywood" gets the blood racing; the word itself is sexy.) Reporters poke microphones through the window of John-Roger's Lexus, the one McWilliams gave the guru in happier days, to ask about John-Roger's ties to Huffington. Sipchen also mentions that McWilliams started taking Prozac after John-Roger demanded royalties on a book the two wrote and McWilliams published.

As his last paragraph to his opening, which runs eight paragraphs, Sipchen writes, "Power, politics, Prozac and Lexuses—if ever there was a tale for the nineties, this was it." As you see, Sipchen hits hard on the hot buttons; as he presents it, this article is also a trend piece. And in what follows, Sipchen tells his tale of the nineties.

Another *Playboy* piece, "Death of a Deceiver," referred to in the previous chapter, uses many of the same elements as Sipchen's story of John-Roger and Peter McWilliams. This article, by Eric Konigsberg, tells the story of Teena Brandon, a young woman who masqueraded as a man and whose secret sexual identity was revealed publicly only upon her murder. Konigsberg sets out to tell you the story behind the story of this minor, regional celebrity, whose celebrity is earned by her previous notoriety.

Unlike a work of fiction or an actual event about which few people know, Konigsberg has to presume that *Playboy* readers have read at least short news reports of this nationally reported story and therefore know at least the bare details of the case; he can't surprise them with the bizarre revelations at the end. So, he gives away the punch line in the first few paragraphs. Konigsberg then starts at the beginning of Brandon's story and relates how and why she played the role of a he, and how this role-playing led to her murder. Once again, the drama and narrative line are built-in; Konigsberg simply tells the story from beginning to end, save for his opening.

There's also lots of sex in this story; without the sex, there would be no story, certainly not for *Playboy*. Brandon was a Doña Juanita in Don Juan's clothing. Dateless as a young woman, Brandon discovered by accident that she could pass for a man, and a man whom innocent teenage girls could not resist. The article basically chronicles Brandon's escapades in seduction, which ended when two former boyfriends of a girl she was dating allegedly murdered her and two other people.

The article is labeled "True Crime," and damned if doesn't read like pulp fiction.

Develop an Ear for Attitude: Tone and Style

Like a fiction writer, a nonfiction writer wields tone, be it ironic or pathetic, as an instrument to convey the writer's perspective.

Let's see how a top journalist, Susan Faludi, does it for *Esquire*. Faludi, who won a Pulitzer Prize while at the *Wall Street Journal* and is author of the best-selling book about the cultural reaction to feminism, *Backlash: The Undeclared War Against American Women*, wrote about men who collect G.I. Joe dolls. She attended the first International G.I. Joe Collectors' Convention. By the use of irony and sarcasm, she demonstrates a certain, shall we say, amused condescension toward grown males who collect military dolls.

In the opening paragraph, she describes a long line of men boarding a mothballed aircraft carrier, the site of the convention. The last sentence of her lead, the punch line in effect, reads: "All, as they approached the checkpoint, were issued the essential equipment for the skirmish ahead on this Saturday morning: Toys R Us shopping bags."

Faludi heightens the sense of the ridiculous with language pertaining to military operations, "issued," "skirmish," and to a lesser degree, "equipment." The adjective "essential" increases the sense of false importance. What Faludi does with this sentence is a common comic device: describing in an overly important way a silly, mundane or unimportant event.

She further belittles the convention with the word "shrimpier" and suggests a crassness with "hawked" in the following sentence: "They maneuvered past tanks and fighter planes, and space capsules to the rows of booths where toy dealers hawked identical, albeit shrimpier tanks, fighter planes and space capsules." A neutral rendition would go something like this: " . . . where toy dealers sold identical, albeit miniature. . . ."

Other examples of Faludi's sarcasm include the sentence, "Occasionally, *in a lapse into reality* [emphasis added], you could find a Joe retooled for the murkier battles of modern times"; and the comment of a woman upon seeing a G.I. Joe bar-brawl diorama with a tiny Rosie the Riveter war poster on the wall: "Oh, look at that: men making a mess of it while women do the actual work."

Notice that Faludi establishes the article's tone not only with language, but also with facts. She probably did not decide to adopt an ironic tone for her article only upon getting back to her office and sitting down to her computer. Faludi had probably already formed an initial opinion about G.I. Joe collectors before attending the convention or perhaps while she was there; one suspects she took on the assignment precisely because the idea of a G.I. Joe collectors' convention sounded a bit loopy and fit in with her interest in sexual politics. This is evident in the little details—the facts—she observes while at the convention and then includes in her piece, once again demonstrating that ideas and research go hand in hand. It's possible that Faludi could record so much minutiae and then cull through it later, but not likely, unless she has a photographic memory. More probably, her mindset drew her to those details and anecdotes that illustrated her point of view after she began to form a conception of what G.I. Joe collecting meant to her.

In keeping with Faludi's tone, and having a little fun at the expense of G.I. Joe collectors, the editors at *Esquire* titled her piece "Guys and Dolls."

Deciding before embarking upon research what kind of tone you want to adopt toward your subject helps guide your research and, in a sense, sharpens the focus of your story. Be advised, however, you do run the risk of passing judgment before all the facts are in. There's much to be said for keeping an open mind; if you make up your mind before gathering all the facts, you might likely intentionally or unintentionally ignore facts that don't support your conclusion. It is possible to do both at once. You can key in on information that supports the thesis you are forming while at the same time remaining open to facts which argue to the contrary.

But as you do research, you should move closer to a sense of what tone you want your article to take. Only once you've finished your research, reflected back upon it, organized it, and thought about it again, however, will a clear sense of approach and tone emerge. And then you'll likely refine it, and sometimes rethink it entirely, when you write the piece itself.

You must also keep in mind that the publication in which you want to place your piece is the ultimate arbiter of tone and style. Is it hip sophistication they want, like *Details*, or friendly, homey warmth a la the *Saturday Evening Post*? Having a sense of the style and tone you want for an article helps further shape your idea for the piece and helps structure your research. Your article will probably come through to readers and editors as authentic if you write the story as honestly as you see it and in the tone that reflects your attitude toward it.

CHAPTER FOUR

The Importance of Research and Approaches to Research

I regard (reporting) as the most valuable and least understood resource available to any writer with exalted ambitions.—Tom Wolfe

I shall always confine myself to the truth, except when it is attended with inconvenience.—Mark Twain, a statement of journalistic principles

Ask the average person on the street what a writer does, and the answer will likely be, after perhaps a perplexed look since the question seems to answer itself: A writer writes. Right? Wrong. Or, maybe half right, if that much, when it comes to nonfiction. The other half of the nonfiction equation is research. Even fiction writers at least observe themselves and other people, which is a form of research.

Many nonfiction writers like to think of themselves as writers first, and researchers only when they're forced into it. To most of the world, writing is creative, and thus glamorous and romantic (most of the world ignores the unpleasant part of planting butt to seat and actually writing), while fact gathering is drudge work. Better to spend time on the well-turned phrase than ferreting out dry bits of information, the tonnage of sheep's wool sheared annually in Australia, for instance.

And the worst part is every nonfiction article is lousy with facts. There are literally hundreds of them in the average newspaper or magazine article, and they all have to be checked, and in many cases double-

and triple-checked. It's such a damn nuisance, and there's no appreciation from either readers or editors for the immense job that research entails.

Readers, and some editors, coo over good writing but take information gathering for granted. But information is the cake of nonfiction, or the substance, while writing style is the icing. And if you've ever watched children eat cake, or ever been one, a child or a piece of cake, you'll notice they invariably eat the tastiest part first: the icing. But without the cake there would be no icing.

Whether they realize it, readers presume the facts that substantiate the novel ideas and situations they expect to read in magazine articles. Readers may say, "Great story!" and "Beautifully written!" but they rarely say, "Awesome research!" Still, it takes the awesome research to make the great story. Think of an article as a circus acrobatic act. You make it look easy with stylish writing, but the hours and days and maybe even weeks of research that provide the tricks or facts for the act—otherwise known as the finished piece—remain largely invisible to the audience.

You can perhaps most readily see nonfictional acrobatics at work in the practitioners of what Tom Wolfe coined New Journalism, now commonly called creative nonfiction. New Journalists were most often cited for their use of fiction techniques, or style as it were, to write nonfiction, but they themselves often commented on how important research was to the success of New Journalism. "You can do all the novelist can do—you just have to do a hell of a lot of research," wrote Gay Talese in 1973. "You have to know your people very, very well."

Wolfe made the same point when people criticized New Journalists for writing what their subjects thought. But they were writing factually, countered Wolfe, because they had asked their subjects, *in great detail*, exactly what they did and said and thought.

Wolfe wrote thusly of New Journalism: "It was more intense, more detailed, and certainly more time-consuming than anything that newspaper or magazine reporters, including investigative reporters, were accustomed to. Only through the most searching forms of reporting was it possible, in nonfiction, to use whole scenes, extended dialogue, point of view, and interior monologue. Eventually I, and others, would be accused of 'entering people's minds'. . . . But exactly! I figured that was one more doorbell a reporter had to push."

Facts Make It Real

As you see, nonfiction is built on facts. Without facts, you have fiction. And though facts are the essence of nonfiction, by definition, facts are more than that. They're the power that makes a story—a *true* story—compelling in a way that fiction cannot make a story compelling. Think about the so-called docudramas that appear on television. Somewhere among the opening credits appears a warning label stating that the program is "based on fact," which everyone interprets to mean that the people who made the program played fast and loose with the truth. That standard proviso has become something of a joke, a standard tool that stand-up comedians use to brand something fake. The reason is fairly simple: People want the genuine article, not an ersatz version. That's why Coke's longtime advertising slogan, "It's the real thing," was so effective.

It's the same with nonfiction writing. Remember Janet Cooke, *The Washington Post* reporter who won a Pulitzer Prize in 1981 for writing a compelling feature about one boy's life in the ghetto? The award was rescinded when it turned out Cooke's story was not fact but based on fact, that is, a composite of several boys' lives. Cooke's transgression crossed the ethical line because she placed no warning label in front of her story. If she had, and published it in a *Post* "Tall Tales" section, the oomph of reality would have gone out of it.

People also don't like being lied to—they don't like being played for fools—and the old saying "stranger than fiction" still has currency. Which is why you not only have to play tight with the truth in your intentions, but also why you must research your story carefully and thoroughly to make sure all the facts are correct. A journalist's reputation is built on credibility. Janet Cooke's was destroyed, and her bright star faded into journalistic oblivion.

Facts Determine the Story

Facts play a more central role in any one story than simply creating the impact of reality. The facts of a story determine what the story is, and they determine a story's structure. They are not simply, after you've gathered enough of them, the ready-mix concrete to pour into the mold of your preconceived notions. You really don't know what your story is and how it will play out in the writing until you've gathered and evaluated all the facts (and even after writing the article you may come to no definitive conclusion).

Take the example of nonfiction writer Fred Setterberg and his research for his collection of travel stories, *The Roads Taken*, which was awarded first place for creative nonfiction in a national competition sponsored by university creative writing programs throughout the country. Setterberg's conceit for his articles, several of which appeared in literary magazines prior to publication in book form, was to travel to various locales associated with great American writers and then write of his experiences as informed by those writers.

"My personal story incubated in the midst of several points having to do with research," Setterberg explains. "Before I went to Nebraska, I read Willa Cather's work and critical studies of Cather. I also read about the history of Nebraska and talked to people who had lived in the Midwest.

"When I went to Nebraska I could experience it backed with some understanding of Cather and her place in Nebraska culture. I was better able to see and understand the Midwestern Gothic sensibility, that darkness in the Midwest you also read in Cather; the Midwest is not just this Norman Rockwell Americana. My research rubbed up against my own experience of it and the two things sparked to create something new, which resulted in my story. That happened in every chapter."

Gathering as much information as you can about a subject gives you, the writer, a greater depth of understanding into your story, even if, as is common, you use in your article only a fraction of the information you've gathered. A huge store of background information allows you to argue convincingly for your article's point of view. The bulk of Setterberg's research, for example, remained largely invisible from public view in his finished pieces, though it hugely influenced his selection and presentation of material.

Setterberg's Cather-colored perception of Nebraska induced him to introduce elements such as Nebraska's infamous serial killer of the late 1950s, Charlie Starkweather. He relates a dinner conversation, of which Starkweather is the main topic of conversation, and he includes the following passage: "When Bruce Springsteen released *Nebraska* [his somber acoustic album with the black-and-white cover photo, whose title song concludes with Charlie Starkweather's soul being hurled into the 'great void' via the state penitentiary's electric chair], the singer explained that he'd fallen under the influence of Flannery O'Connor's short stories. But Springsteen could have read Willa Cather to the same effect."

Setterberg's sense of Midwestern Gothic Nebraska resonates in the piece's final passage. Setterberg and his wife, Ann, discover the commercial meat locker to which his wife's grandfather had taken her many years before when she was a little girl.

"Inside the refrigerated vault," Setterberg writes, "we found a whole scalded pig and marbled strips of beef dangling upon their sharpened metal hooks. The locker felt unbearably chilly. It stank of blood, flesh and refrigerated air. Ann turned to me, grinned innocently and said, 'It's funny what you can't forget.' "

Imagine Setterberg had done much less book research, say reading perhaps one of Cather's books and looking up "Cather" and "Nebraska" in an encyclopedia, or maybe reading nothing more than a travel guidebook. His story would then primarily rest on his experience of Nebraska with little literary or historical context, more likely a one-dimensional account of Nebraska rather than the fully dimensional one he created with its nuances and shadings.

Even worse than not getting the full dimensions of a story, thanks to insufficient research, a writer can blunder and miss the story or get it all wrong. Writers gather way more information on their subject than they use in their story precisely to make sure they don't posit a theme that those knowledgeable on the subject could easily expose as ridiculous. Nor do they want to overlook important facts.

An abundance of facts gained through research also strengthens your story with the information that finds its way into your finished piece. See how much more complete and convincing a personality profile is when you interview and then quote friends and foes of the profile subject rather than merely interviewing the subject and including some brief, biographical material? Or quoting three or four or five different experts or sources rather than one to make your points in an article about, say, the efficacy of a new and controversial medical treatment?

Research also shapes and structures stories. Setterberg wove his three major strands of research—writer, place and personal experience—into every story. They constituted the framework upon which his stories were built, with one or two strands playing a more prominent role than the others at any one point in the story.

In "Underneath Willa Cather's Nebraska," the story's first section mentions Cather, but it is mostly about the land, his reaction to it and his wife's reaction mixed with her memory of growing up there. After telling about the time Ann and her grandmother look at the grandmother's wedding dress in the attic, Setterberg writes: "Now when Ann thinks back on that summer afternoon when they unwound the delicate lace and let it flutter to the floor, she realizes that her grandmother probably had not been daydreaming at all about some child's future wedding; she'd been reliving her own. Much of Nebraska, Ann insisted, was like the dress resurrected in the dim attic light: some dream of passion stored away for decades, only now and then privately revived.

"As we drove south through the barbed whiskers of wheat and corn, I began to grasp what she meant. It was certainly possible to write off the countryside as an interminable plain. ('The only thing very noticeable about Nebraska,' admonished Willa Cather's worried narrator in the opening pages of *My Antonia*, 'was that it was still, all day, Nebraska.') But by the time we'd reached the middle of the state, the dead sea of flat, sprawling land had lapped up upon itself in foamy waves of bristling alfalfa and sugar beets to form one of the most gorgeous landscapes I'd ever seen."

The second section focuses on Cather: "The Cather family first moved to Red Cloud in 1884. Young Willa wanted to leave immediately, missing the forests surrounding her family's old Virginia farm .... But over time, Willa found that the landscape of her new home whipped up in her an adolescent passion to which she could surrender with all the heat and single-mindedness of first love."

The third with experience: the indifferent, mistaken notions of the Midwest in general and Nebraska in particular by Americans who live along the nation's coasts.

The concluding section returns to the couple's direct experience in Nebraska, a return to Ann's grandparents' home and the previously mentioned meat locker episode. Cather is brought into the piece throughout and certainly informs it, but she really only takes center stage in the second section.

Gathering a plenitude of individual facts for a story also gives you options when you sit down to write. Options can affect a story's flow. One quote or anecdote might work better than others to illustrate a point at a certain place in your story, while you can plug in the others elsewhere. A specific quote, anecdote or discrete fact can provide the transition to another part of your story. (See my own anecdote in the next section for an example.)

The order in which you do your research also makes a difference in the finished piece. As Setterberg points out, the order in which he researched Nebraska and Willa Cather, that is, background and book research first and field research second, was vital to writing about his wife's upbringing in Nebraska and their travels in the state. There is a danger, however, to doing background research first and field research second: you may form preconceptions that blind you to other possible interpretations; you may ignore facts that fall outside the scenario you've already imagined. The antidote: Keep your mind open and test your theories against all the information you uncover.

In a relatively short amount of time, you must make yourself a credible specialist in your subject. Editors invariably call with follow-up questions to your submitted piece, and they're a lot more impressed with writers who can quickly supply the answers than those who respond, "I don't know." Confusion, lack of clarity and unanswered questions that pop into the reader's mind break the spell that you as the writer want to cast, even in purely informational articles.

Provide your reader with a smooth, unobstructed road to the end of your piece. Fill all potholes and eliminate all roadblocks and detours. A confused reader quickly loses interest. There are exceptions, however, on the most sophisticated level. There are times when you want to provoke the reader with consciously wrought contradictions and unanswered questions inherent in your story. But don't confuse the reader needlessly with unanswered questions for which there are ready answers.

Are We Having Fun Yet?

So the ugly fact remains unavoidable: Facts are the essence of nonfiction, and somebody—you—is going to have to go out and get them. Now here's a secret few non-nonfiction writers know: Research is fun, and for many nonfiction writers it's more fun than writing the story. Research is so much fun it can become an addiction. With research, you avoid writing, an activity many writers engage in only after energetic resistance; it takes a lot of heavy mental lifting to make sense of the information you gather, to organize it so it makes sense to the reader and then to write clear, convincing and even stylish sentences.

More seriously, perhaps, research is fun because it feeds the insatiable curiosity most writers possess; they went into journalism to find out about stuff. Searching for information is a lot like playing detective. You hunt for something—information—and with it you solve a mystery. The biggest problem with research for many nonfiction writers is not that they have to do it but that they have to stop doing it, even when they know they've done enough. The esteemed and reviled gonzo journalist, Hunter S. Thompson, whose celebrity has been institutionalized in newspaper comic pages throughout the country as Uncle Duke in *Doonesbury*, frequently blamed the exigencies of "research" for his outrageous, and at times illegal, behavior.

Once while doing research for the introduction to a travel guidebook on California, I read in a handful of books that President Teddy Roosevelt had characterized California as "west of the West." I liked the phrase and wanted to quote Roosevelt, but I wanted to bring something new to it since other writers had used it. Mostly, however, I was just curious about the circumstances under which Roosevelt made the statement.

I tracked the original quote to a book in the California history room at the University of California, Berkeley, library. The book recounted Roosevelt's two-week trip to California in 1903. I found a superb anecdote: the trip itself, but more specifically a speech Roosevelt made to a group of prominent San Franciscans. Even around the turn of the century, I was fascinated to discover in Roosevelt's speech that Americans harbored an ambivalence about California. Roosevelt, a tourist of sorts himself—he camped in the Sierra Nevada Mountains with environmentalist John Muir—alluded to this ambivalence in his speech:

"While I am not by inheritance a Puritan, I have acquired certain traits, one of which is an uneasy feeling which I think a large number of Americans share, that when we are having a good time, it is not quite right [laughter and applause]. And during the week I have been in California I have enjoyed myself so much that I have had a slight feeling that maybe I was not quite doing my duty [applause]. But I cannot say that I am penitent about it."

I immediately knew I had struck gold; what a terrific option research had presented me. I had as my ending Roosevelt's San Francisco speech and that quote. Now, I also had my beginning. I opened with the following lead:

"Of the many things said about California, Teddy Roosevelt perhaps said it best. In 1903, during a swing through the state, the nation's twenty-sixth president told the assembled citizenry of Ventura, 'When I come to California, I am not in the West. I am west of the West.'"

Roosevelt's quote provided me a springboard to launch into a discussion about the literal and metaphorical roles California has played in American culture. Eventually, I worked my way to his San Francisco speech, and so I tied up my introduction in one neat package, thanks to my natural curiosity and penchant to dig deeper.

Approaches to Research: Research Strategies

Here's the nondirected approach to researching a story: You run out and get your hands on everything ever printed on the subject and talk to as many people as possible. Depending on the story, you may eventually have to leave no stone unturned. But you'll save yourself a lot of time and effort if first you devise a research strategy. Fortunately, the approach falls along some predictable lines.

Let's presume your story is the typical magazine feature or department piece, and that you're doing preliminary research, perhaps in preparation to write a story proposal. You might call a source or two in government, business, or an association or special interest group for a few basics facts. You might also check some statistics in a report or reference book. But early on, maybe as the very first step, you nearly always want to check newspaper and magazine articles. If any exist on your subject, and it's a good bet they do, they'll supply you with an overview and a few basic facts. Moreover, they'll tell you what the competition has already done. You can then think up a new angle and pitch your proposal to the appropriate markets, i.e., magazines other than the ones that have already published similar pieces.

The desirable exception to this typical pattern is if you already know your subject in-depth, either because you have a burning interest in the story and have already thoroughly researched it, or you're a specialist in a field and so possess in-depth knowledge about any number of as of yet unpublished stories. You obviously can skip the preliminary research, and you probably already know what's been published on the subject.

Once you get the assignment, your research is limited by your time and resources, and the story's intrinsic demands. More ambitious stories, that is, ones that are typically longer and more in-depth, demand more research. You'll almost always start to dig deeper. Presumably, in order to have written your proposal, you already will have determined your story's scope. You should know before you start researching approximately how much and what kind of material you'll need. Your research may lead to a larger story, but you can save that story for another publication, or maybe a book (lots of books have grown out of magazine articles). You might also go back to your editor and pitch the larger story.

As your research proceeds, you'll gather more documentary evidence at the library, online or from private sources; and you'll venture into the field to interview people and observe situations firsthand. In general, here are the bases you'd typically cover for in-depth research: articles; books; reports; reference sources such as encyclopedias, dictionaries, directories and indices; original documentary sources such as public records and private papers; and original nondocumentary sources such as interviews and field observations. Shorter pieces may only require talking to a few people on the telephone and checking a few facts. Within a few hours, you've gathered enough information to write a short item or a department piece.

With a longer, interpretative story, however, one in which you try to understand and interpret for the reader an issue, event or profile subject, a few additional research steps are required. The drill works something like this: You gather all the information you think is necessary to write the story; you evaluate your information; you go back and get more information to fill in the gaps and clear up any puzzling aspects; then you sit down to write the piece and check a bit more as new questions arise.

This more involved approach to research lets you make the most informed judgment you can about your story. If the story starts to write itself inside your head anytime while you're doing research, give in to the urge and write it down. Just reserve judgment until the end. Those words born of inspiration may very well find their way into your finished piece. On the other hand, you may finally decide they were ill-conceived, and you'll discard them.

Gathering all your information first rather than, say, getting information for one part of your story, writing it and then moving on to the next, also has the advantage of detecting research snags and road-blocks sooner than later, which gives you a better chance to deal with them. How are you to know that your key expert plans to slog through the Amazon rain forest, miles from a telephone, for an entire month unless you check as soon as possible?

On occasion, a deadline looms too near for you to construct your story in the most desirable, logical way. If you run into snags and must wait for information—that expert you need to talk to is in Sweden accepting a Nobel prize and has no time for your interview—go ahead and start writing the parts of your story for which you have the information, and revise as more information becomes available.

For discrete information, that is a specific fact or figure, rely first on reference sources: directories, indexes, encyclopedias and specialized dictionaries. Rare is the fact you can't find in a reference source. Also, don't hesitate to telephone the reference desk at your local library; the librarians there often will look up answers to specific questions.

And last but not least, use the telephone freely. Other than your own mind, it's your most precious resource for nonfiction writing. You can accomplish in minutes by telephone what might otherwise take days. Call people first to arrange interviews; call experts for information and informed opinions; call the reference librarian for individual facts. Many writers use the telephone so much they invest in an operator's headset.

The Need to Read

Research is ongoing and not specific to any one story. Your natural curiosity should drive you to read constantly from a wide variety of sources. It's amazing what tidbits of information you can pick up by serendipity. In chapter two, for example, I used as an example of an *Atlantic Monthly* article about the nation's marijuana enforcement policies. A week or two after writing that paragraph, I read an article in *The New York Times*, which I read daily, about the National Magazine Awards for 1994. The news story mentioned that the article won that year's award for reporting. I included this bit of information to give my example greater authority. I saw no story on the awards in my local newspaper, the *San Francisco Chronicle*.

CHAPTER FIVE

The (Mostly) Paper Trail: Library Research, Government Documents, Public Records, Private Sources

My library was dukedom large enough.—William Shakespeare, *The Tempest*

No place affords a more striking conviction of the vanity of human hopes than a public library.—Samuel Johnson

You remember the scenario from your school days, or if you're still in school, think back to last week. The teacher assigns you a report, and as if on automatic pilot you go to the library to gather the information you need. Or perhaps as a young child you asked your parents or some other adult a question like the one from the old Bill Cosby comedy routine, "Why is there air?" and they fended you off under the guise of instilling self-reliance: Look it up!

Now that you're all grown up and voluntarily, eagerly, writing reports otherwise known as nonfiction articles, you find things haven't changed much. You think of an idea for a story, and it's back to the old school routine. You go the library; you look it up.

At the Library. But Which Library?
With home references, such as encyclopedias, almanacs and dictionaries, you might check individual facts or perhaps take a very preliminary look at a subject for a potential story, but very quickly you're going

to have to get yourself down to the library for some serious research. In your elementary, junior high or high school days, that meant the public library. And if you've pursued a degree in higher education, you know that a college or university library typically holds far more information than the local public library. But what you might not know is that there are a few other kinds of libraries at your disposal. They exist because they have specialized purposes and so carry specialized material. Here's a rundown on a few kinds of libraries, familiar and unfamiliar.

Public Libraries

Contrary to popular opinion, the public library is not a place that houses books, at least not *exclusively*. There's even more to the public library than newspapers and magazines. Nowadays, libraries also lend videocassettes and audio recordings on vinyl, cassette tapes and compact discs. They contain maps, pamphlets and all kinds of statistical information on microfilm, microfiche and CD-ROM. Many major public libraries maintain history rooms containing region-specific historical information. And some libraries maintain computer terminals with Internet connections so you can go online and search for information in cyberspace.

Like the rest of the world, libraries are becoming increasingly computerized. In fact, long ago librarians understood the perfect fit of computers and the formidable task of cataloging vast amounts of information. Library computerization has now filtered down to the patrons, and will probably continue into the foreseeable future. Many libraries not only maintain computerized catalogs, once known as the card catalog, but they also maintain many of their reference works, such as directories and indices, and much of their statistical information as search services on CD-ROM. When it comes to library research, the computer is an incredibly powerful tool. So if you count yourself among the computer challenged, get over it! Because the sooner you learn computing, the more effective a researcher you'll be.

Public librarians can assist you in your research in several ways, and often over the telephone. They can make sure a book the computerized catalog says is in is actually on the shelves. They can put a hold on the book, or a book that's checked out, and arrange for you to pick it up at the front desk. They can arrange for you to borrow a book through an interlibrary loan. They'll even take phone requests for answers to specific research questions.

Interlibrary loan deserves special mention. It's your way to expand your library's lending capacity way beyond the library's own collection. Approximately six thousand public and academic libraries nationwide participate in an online database that catalogs the libraries' holdings. Think of it as one immense card catalog. Ask your local librarian for a book or periodical article by author and title, and the computer search of OCLC (Online Computer Library Center, Inc.) finds and displays the names of libraries housing the information you need. The librarian then requests the material through OCLC. It may take a week or two to fulfill your request. With libraries still sending interlibrary loan requests by conventional mail, the process might take a month or two or even longer. Ask the usual turnaround time, and then check back with your local library if the materials don't arrive within the allotted time.

As you can see, there's a lot more to the public library than books.

Business Libraries

Most metropolitan library systems have one branch dedicated to business, otherwise known as the business library. Business libraries, often located near a city's business district, operate like any other branch except they carry a much more extensive collection of books and periodicals pertaining to business. A business library is an excellent resource not only for working on business-related stories, but also for locating companies and researching consumer buying patterns that may suggest a cultural trend. Check the business library's operating times, as it may keep business hours.

Academic Libraries

If you want to see the work product of all those academics who, in their quest for academia's Holy Grail, otherwise known as tenure, must publish or perish, go to a college library. There reside academic journals and scholarly texts of every stripe, along with the theses and dissertations of the school's own graduate students. These books, journals and papers, dry as they may be in the reading, represent a deluge of in-depth information on often very narrow topics in specialized fields. In short, they're probably the richest source of expert information available in one place. Academic libraries also, of course, contain vast numbers of books and periodicals that were not created under the aegis of academia. You almost always find much more of what you want in a university library than a big-city library. Community college libraries collect large amounts of vocational information, in say real estate, construction and police and fire science.

Academic libraries vary on how much access they allow the general public. Some extend borrowing privileges to residents of the surrounding community while others may allow members of the public to use their materials only on-site. Still others may place certain sections off limits. It's unusual, especially with public colleges and universities, that the public is banned outright. College libraries usually keep longer hours than public libraries, so you can spend night after night researching your story.

Historical Society Libraries

Historical society libraries can prove invaluable resources, and in many cases the only resources, when it comes to researching the history of specific regions. Oftentimes, they house original material such as old letters, diaries, family histories, local newspapers, minutes of meetings, company records and photographs. Historical societies, which often depend solely on donations and volunteer help, vary greatly in the size of their collections. Sometimes access to their libraries may require membership in the society, but usually an earnest research request, by mail, telephone or in person, will be met with cheerful assistance. After all, that's what the libraries are there for.

Company Libraries

Major corporations often maintain libraries to help employees do their jobs better. Many don't want to waste their time dealing with the public, but others are willing to fulfill research requests, especially if you can convince the librarian, or better yet the public relations officer, that your story will reap publicity benefits for the company. Company librarians can often steer you toward authoritative books and leading experts in a particular subject that pertains to the company's business.

If your story involves in-depth research into a specific company's history or the history of an industry in which that company is a major player, or if you need the answer to an arcane question about a specific company or industry, put a corporation library on your research itinerary.

Government Depository Libraries

By law, certain libraries throughout a state are designated federal government depository libraries. These libraries receive heaps of federal reports and documents deemed to have educational value or public interest. This is where you go to get U.S. census statistical information (information on individuals by name are available from the National Archives) and the full texts of contemporary federal laws and regulations (some depositories don't contain the texts of laws enacted many years ago). Depository libraries also contain federal directories and indices, government-compiled statistical reports on labor, business and industry, and the innumerable books and magazines published by the U.S. Government, which, by the way, is the nation's largest publisher. Approximately fourteen hundred government depository libraries are located throughout the country, usually at least one in each congressional district and usually as part of an academic or large public library.

Specialized Libraries and Research Centers

In addition to the basic kinds of libraries discussed above, numerous libraries and research centers open to public inquiries run the gamut from art museum libraries to zoological society research centers. To find in-house research centers, check *Research Centers Directory*. To find the full scope of libraries nationwide, check *Directory of Special Libraries and Information Centers* (public and academic libraries are included). Both are published by Gale Research Company. *Subject Collections*, published by R.R. Bowker Company, covers by subject the collections of about seven thousand public, academic, museum and historical society libraries in the U.S.

Library Research

The research methods and resources discussed in this section focus on the public library, since that's where you'll do the majority of your research, but you'll find that they basically apply to other libraries as well. Note that many reference resources listed below such as master indices are guides to other guides, which may only list the location of the information you ultimately want.

Also, pay attention to whether a resource is a resource of titles, such as newspaper and periodical indices, which tell you what publication contains the article you want, or whether the resource actually contains the information you're seeking, such as encyclopedias, dictionaries and directories—unless the directory is a directory of directories—which in fact was the name of one such directory until the name was recently changed. (" 'Curiouser and curiouser!' cried Alice. . . . ") Don't worry. It's not as confusing as it sounds once you root around on your own. And feel free to enlist the help of your friendly librarian.

Finding Books

The card catalog is, of course, your road map to the books on your library's shelves. To remind you of what you probably know, you can search for a book by subject, title or author. Fiction is arranged on the shelves by the author's last name; nonfiction according to a book's call number, which is based on the Library of Congress or Dewey Decimal classification system.

Computerized cataloging, the wave of the archival future, also indexes books according to subject, title and author. But unlike the card catalog, in which you must conform subject searches to the catalog's categories, you perform a computerized subject search by typing in keywords. The result is a customized, and therefore quicker and more efficient, search. You also don't need exact titles, only a key word or two of a title. In addition, the computer gathers and displays the information much quicker than you can do using the card catalog.

If computerized catalog searching isn't nifty enough already as compared to card catalogs, you can often do it from home. I checked on many of the books mentioned in this chapter by accessing my local library's computerized catalog from my home computer, and through the library's Internet connection (an option on the catalog screen), I checked the University of California's computerized book catalog as well. I saved the information on my computer's internal hard drive as the information appeared on the screen, and have it for ready reference. I accomplished in about an hour what otherwise, factoring in travel time, would have taken the better part of a day. Talk about time savers. . . .

To look for books beyond your local library without the benefit of computer and modem, turn to the multivolume *Books in Print*, published by R.R. Bowker Company. Other than the Library of Congress's own catalog, this is the last word on books published in the U.S. The main library in any locality, and some branches as well, should carry it. Updated annually, *Books in Print* is divided into three sets: subject, title and author. The title and author sets cover fiction and nonfiction; the subject guide covers nonfiction except for multiauthor, fiction collections. Since *Books in Print* is primarily a reference source on book publishing, the listings show a book's publisher, not where to find a book in libraries. Note that libraries house lots of books out of print, so don't think *Books in Print* lists every book out there. Still, it is an excellent resource for finding books on your subject.

The card catalog and *Books in Print* won't help you when it comes to finding chapters in anthologies. For that task, consult *Essay and General Literature Index*, published by H.W. Wilson. This is a subject index that lists the author, chapter description and book title. The index is particularly effective in guiding you to works on subjects that appear unrelated to their anthology titles.

Reference books constitute the precious resources of libraries. You know this because reference books are usually the books libraries won't let you take home. Take a copy of *Moby Dick* if you want, take two, but forget about the multivolume *Books in Print*, even if you could carry it off without giving yourself a hernia. That said, you might try a few loopholes. Some libraries, for instance make overnight loans of certain reference books, while others keep duplicate or previous editions of reference books in storage. One reference book I wanted for my research for this book, *The Reporter's Handbook: An Investigator's Guide to Documents and Techniques*, was located in the science and business department of my local library, behind the desk, not even on the shelves—a precious resource indeed! A second copy was in storage. I got to take that one home.

For a bibliography of reference books and a guide to library reference services, check *Where to Find What: A Handbook to Reference Service*, by James M. Hillard, Scarecrow Press.

To find the names, addresses and telephone numbers of American and Canadian book publishers, literary agents and publishing publicity sources, check *Literary Market Place*, produced by R.R. Bowker Company.

Finding Articles

Those not up to snuff with the latest in library search tools will likely turn to *Reader's Guide to Periodical Literature* to find bibliographic information on magazine articles. Unfortunately, even some libraries are not up snuff with the latest in library technology, so they don't have the computer terminals that contain InfoTrac or other such article-search services. Fortunately, most main public libraries in large and medium-size cities do.

Most libraries that carry InfoTrac supply at least two of Information Access Corp's several databases: *Magazine Index Plus* and *National Newspaper Index*. *Magazine Index Plus* indexes bibliographic information on articles from about four hundred general interest magazines most commonly found in public libraries, along with the current two months of *The New York Times*, *Wall Street Journal* and *Christian Science Monitor*. Many of the indexed articles include abstracts, that is, brief descriptions about the articles. *National Newspaper Index* indexes *The New York Times*, *Wall Street Journal*, *Christian Science Monitor*, *The Washington Post* and *Los Angeles Times*. Some public libraries may carry a combination of the two indices, called *General Periodicals Index*, and some libraries may additionally carry *Business Index*, which consists of an article bibliography of more than seven hundred business, management and trade periodicals. Two other Info-Trac bibliographies you might find are *Health Index*, which thoroughly indexes about 150 core publications in health and medicine, with selective indexing of twenty-five hundred other titles; and *Legal-Trac*, which indexes articles of more than eight hundred legal publications. InfoTrac also produces databases with the full text of articles.

You can search through InfoTrac bibliographies by subject or key title words. The libraries often have printers connected to their computer terminals, so you can print out the bibliographic information you find. The InfoTrac bibliographies cover three full years plus however many months of the current year, and are updated monthly. Some libraries place their InfoTrac databases online along with their electronic catalogs, so you can search from home with your computer and modem.

Reader's Guide indexes the articles of about 180 popular periodicals updated biweekly, a tiny fraction of the approximately 147,000 publications listed in *Ulrich's International Periodicals Directory*. Small libraries may only carry *Reader's Guide*. Large libraries may carry not only InfoTrac, which in itself will only get you so far, but also specialized indices covering articles of periodicals focusing on specific religions, ethnic groups, geographic regions or areas of human endeavor such as politics and sports.

To find out which indices handle the articles of a specific magazine, check *Ulrich's*, or the smaller *Magazines for Libraries*, published by R.R. Bowker Company.

A few specialized indices you might find useful are the following:

Population Index, Office of Population Research, Population Association of America, Inc., and Princeton University, covers about five hundred periodicals on demographics and population trends.

Index Medicus, National Library of Medicine, covers some twenty-six hundred international, professional and scholarly journals in medical research and treatment.

Humanities Index, H.W. Wilson Company, covers more than two hundred periodicals focusing on fields such as history, literature, politics, philosophy, theology, language and performing arts.

Social Sciences Index, H.W. Wilson Company, covers more than 250 periodicals in a broad array of fields, including criminology, public administration and environmental studies.

Writings on American History, American Historical Association, covers about four hundred periodicals focusing on the American history of culture, business, industry, religion and the arts, among other topics.

International Political Science Abstracts, International Political Science Association, covers some seven hundred periodicals on political philosophy, military policy, foreign policy and international relations.

Index to United States Government Periodicals, Infordata International Inc., covers the federal government's 170 or so periodicals, which range from scientific and sociological research to national defense, the arts, and wildlife and conservation.

The following are directories of publications. Unlike the subject indices listed above, these directories provide information about the publications themselves—names, addresses, focus of interest, sometimes editors—*not* article titles. These directories are useful for finding publications on specific subjects, but sometimes the listings are outdated.

Ulrich's International Periodicals Directory, R.R. Bowker Company, is, as alluded to above, the most comprehensive directory of publications internationally, including the United States and Canada. Some 147,000 publications with names, addresses and phone numbers are listed under 967 subject headings.

Gale Directory of Publications and Broadcast Media, Gale Research Company, is indispensable for finding information on newspapers, journals and magazines in the U.S. and Canada. It lists by region thirty-eight thousand publication names, including addresses, voice and fax telephone numbers, circulation, frequency of publication and the names of each publication's publisher and primary editor. A separate volume contains indices by subject and by publication name. Newspaper feature editors are also listed.

National Directory of Newsletters and Reporting Services, Gale Research Company, is a reference guide to national and international financial, educational and informational services, and association newsletters.

Finding Info-bites: Encyclopedias and Dictionaries

Encyclopedias provide an overview of a subject and often a short bibliography for further reading; they're a good first stop when researching a story. Sometimes they're also the quickest way to check on a single fact. General interest encyclopedias vary widely in their scope and depth, so compare encyclopedias to determine which is best for your purpose.

General interest encyclopedias constitute only the tip of the encyclopedia iceberg, however. Subject-specific encyclopedias are much more useful to the nonfiction researcher. You'll find entries you won't find in a general interest encyclopedia, and you'll usually find more in-depth coverage of a subject both books might cover. In addition, you'll probably find a longer recommended bibliography for each subject. Like subject-specific encyclopedias, subject-specific dictionaries put a wealth of information about a single field at your fingertips. Legal and medical dictionaries usually consist of a single volume, nevertheless they explain an entry in more detail than a common, English language dictionary, and of course carry many more subject-specific definitions.

To find encyclopedias and dictionaries that suit your needs, check Eugene P. Sheehy's *Guide to Reference Books*, published by American Library Association. It contains an excellent, annotated listing of specialized dictionaries and encyclopedias, both national and international, categorized by broad subject areas such as humanities; history; social and behavioral sciences; and science, technology and medicine. Also check *Subject Guide to Books in Print*. For subject-specific references in your local library, check your library's catalog under your subject cross-referenced with "encyclopedias," "dictionaries," "directories" or "indices." You'll be surprised to find encyclopedia-like books on very narrow topics.

Listed below are a few encyclopedic resources you might find useful; they also give you an idea of what's out there:

> *Encyclopedia of Education*, Macmillan.
> *Encyclopaedia of Religion and Ethics*, C. Scribner's Sons.
> *Encyclopedia of World Art*, McGraw-Hill.
> *International Encyclopedia of the Social Sciences*, Macmillan.
> *McGraw-Hill Encyclopedia of Science and Technology*, McGraw-Hill.
> *New Grove Dictionary of Music and Musicians*, Macmillan.
> *Black's Law Dictionary*, West Publishing Company.
> *Taber's Cyclopedic Medical Dictionary*, F.A. Davis Company.

Finding People and Organizations; Facts and Figures

There are enough facts in the world to fill all the world's oceans three times over, and if stacked on top of one another, they'd reach to Saturn's rings. There are an equal number of factoids in the world, probably more when you account for human error and the penchant for lying. Fortunately for you the researcher, you'll find just the facts, or where to go to find the facts, in the numerous compendiums kept in your local libraries (an occasional factoid does slip in; people compile these compendiums, after all). Use the following resources to locate a person, organization or company, but keep in mind, as the first listing spells out, there are thousands more resources than the few I've listed here. If your library doesn't stock the exact title, ask if there's another one that will do the job.

People and Organizations
> *Biography and Genealogy Master Index*, and its larger counterpart in microform, *Bio-base*, Gale Research Co., are your keys to

more than three million biographical sketches contained in some 350 biographical dictionaries. The biography master indices duplicate six other Gale biographical master indices, known in the library trade as BMIs: authors, children's authors and illustrators, writers for young adults, journalists, performing artists and historical figures. You look up the name of the person you're interested in either in the master master index or the master index (not all libraries keep the multivolume master master) and then go to the appropriate directory to read a biographical sketch.

Biography Index, H.W. Wilson Co., indexes biographical article titles in a wide variety of fields from about two thousand popular and scholarly periodicals, along with biographical books and book chapters.

Current Biography, H.W. Wilson Co, issued monthly and cumulated annually, contains biographical summaries of about twenty-five hundred words on contemporary national and international newsmakers. About 150 biographies are collected annually, and obituaries are updated. It also indexes articles on newsmakers.

Webster's Biographical Dictionary, Merriam Company, contains short, biographical sketches on upwards of forty thousand nationally and internationally notable persons, living and dead.

Marquis Who's Who Publications: Index to All Books, Marquis Who's Who Inc., indexes the more than a dozen *Who's Who* books, the old, school report stalwarts that provide biographical sketches on famous people. *Who's Who* books are categorized by region or by areas such as government or religion. Look up the name to find out which book contains the biographical sketch. *Who's Who* books provide a decent, preliminary overview of a person's life, and many libraries carry *Who's Who*, but be aware that the biographical sketches are really autobiographical sketches, or at least authorized biographical sketches; the biographical subjects wield the blue pencil when it comes to their own write-ups.

Directories in Print, published by Gale Research Company. This mother of all directories is a directory of directories (its previous name) to business and professional people and organizations. The directory provides an alphabetized list of more than ten thousand international directories with the names, addresses and telephone numbers of the publishers. Since many specialized directories are published by business and professional organizations, you may need look only as far as *Directories in Print* to find an organization specializing in your chosen subject. It also contains a separate volume with a subject index and a title and keyword index.

Company ProFile, Information Access Company, is a CD-ROM database that lists by name more than one hundred thousand private and public companies, including addresses, telephone numbers, a brief description of the company and names of key officers. Depending on what IAC databases your local library buys, you can probably access this database and IAC's newspaper and magazine databases from a single computer terminal.

Standard & Poor's Register of Corporations, Directors and Executives, Standard & Poor's Corp., alphabetically lists thirty-seven thousand U.S. corporations in volume one, and includes the names of directors and key executives; lists alphabetically in volume two the directors and executives of those thirty-seven thousand corporations; and in volume three categorizes the corporations geographically and by product.

Telephone, Criss-Cross and City Directories, These are three similar kinds of directories listing names, addresses and telephone numbers. Your local main library usually has telephone directories for many populous areas outside your locale. Try looking in the white or yellow pages first for some person or business you want to track down before turning to convoluted methods. The *Criss-Cross Directory* for a city, usually published by Haines and Company, lists names and telephone numbers by address. Reporters wanting to talk surreptitiously with the neighbors of a story's subject often turn to the *Criss-Cross Directory*. Since many people no longer list their addresses or full names, these directories are less useful than they once were. They also may contain dated information. City directories mainly give you a window to the past, as few if any of these directories are still published. *City Directories of the United States*, published in microform by Research Publications, Inc., reproduces dozens of city directories from the mid-eighteenth century to 1901. The guide to the microform, *Bibliography of American Directories Through 1860,* is a book printed by Greenwood Press. Check your library's card catalog under "city directories" for similar directories published in your area.

Facts and Figures = Statistics

> *American Statistics Index (ASI), Index to International Statistics (IIS)* and *Statistical Reference Index (SRI)*, all published by Congressional Information Service, Inc., collectively compile the titles of more than three thousand statistical directories and numerous statistical reports, not the statistics themselves; you have to go to the source for the numbers. The company produces the indexed material in full text on microform. The information is also available, of course, from the originating sources, often in print. Material not located at your local library is often available through an interlibrary loan.
>
> ASI indexes reports and directories of statistical information generated by federal and state governments, such as the FBI annual report. IIS indexes reports and directories on international issues such as world employment and global energy consumption that are published by bodies such as various United Nations agencies and the International Monetary Fund. SRI indexes the statistical reports and journalistic articles generated by entities such as commercial publishers, businesses, associations, special interest groups and universities.
>
> You use these indices in a two-step fashion. First, look in the index volume (the indices are generated monthly and compiled into annual volumes) under the subject category, which can be a broad topic such as "medical costs" or a locale or organization. Get the report number from the index volume and then look in the abstract volume for a brief description of the report and who published it.
>
> *PAIS International in Print,* Public Affairs Information Service Inc., is a key resource for many reporters covering legislation, public policy and social sciences. It indexes government publications, reports and other documents, including reports of U.S. congressional hearings, as well as commercially published books and periodicals. The emphasis is on material that weighs heavily on statistical and factual information. The book is written in En-

glish, but it covers material published in English, French, German, Italian, Portuguese and Spanish.

Encyclopedia of Business Information Sources, Gale Research Co., is an alternative guide to the indices of statistical publications discussed above. This encyclopedia, though not quite as comprehensive as those indices, also lists under subject headings titles of encyclopedias, dictionaries, biographies, handbooks, manuals and other such references, and includes bibliographies. It is a key resource for researching many kinds of stories, not just business stories.

Statistical Abstract of the United States, produced by the U.S. Department of Commerce and published by the U.S. Government Printing Office, is the Census Bureau's annual compilation of how the United States looks statistically in a myriad of ways. Drawn from studies conducted by various government agencies and private sources, the *Statistical Abstract* is an excellent, one-stop reference source for American statistical information. It covers an incredibly diverse number of subjects, most often presented in statistical tables. Subjects range from general demographic analyses to ice cream consumption to deaths categorized by weapons used to the number of people who visit national parks. It mainly provides a summary of statistical studies, and indexes the titles of the complete studies. Think of it as an encyclopedia of U.S. statistical information.

Statistical Yearbook, United Nations, Department of International Economic and Social Affairs, Statistical Office, takes an annual look at finance, agriculture, manufacturing, mining, construction and other like activities for more than 125 countries. UNESCO, which is associated with the United Nations, also publishes a *Statistical Yearbook* that covers culture, education, science and technology for more than two hundred countries.

National Trade Data Bank, U.S. Department of Commerce, is a CD-ROM that contains a wealth of information on nearly every aspect of trade, including imports and exports.

Federal Government Resources

As mentioned in the section on government depository libraries, federal government-generated information not only informs the citizenry about the government's activities but also about the activities of its citizens and the status of the nation's land and resources. Government publications comprise tremendous resources for researchers. The problem with government information is sifting through the unbelievable mass of it to find the nuggets of informational gold you want. Don't hesitate to ask the government depository librarian for help.

You should find the following written, federal government resources in any large library, not just government depositories. (U.S. Census Bureau information is listed above in the section on finding statistical information.) If you want to buy government publications, including most Census Bureau information, contact the Superintendent of Documents, U.S. Government Printing Office, Washington, DC 20402; telephone: (202) 512-1800.

> *United States Government Manual* provides the most extensive guide to all offices of all branches of the U.S. Government. This manual will help you determine which government office generated a document, a must for Freedom of Information Act requests. It lists departments, agencies and offices and a brief description of the responsibilities of each office, along with key names, addresses and telephone numbers. Some federal government departments make public their internal telephone directories, which provide more names and numbers in the specific department than the *Government Manual.*
>
> *Federal Information Center* is a phone-in, federal government service that answers frequently asked questions about government benefits and services. FIC reps will steer you toward the office or agency that can answer your questions. Centers are located throughout the country; check the phone book for the number in your area.
>
> *Monthly Catalog of U.S. Government Publications* is the primary guide to federal publications and reports even though it lists less than an estimated half of all federal publications. Collected into annual volumes, the catalog indexes publications' subject, title, author and series or report numbers. It also includes a publication's GPO number, which you'll need along with the title if you want to buy the publication from the Superintendent of Documents; and it shows whether the publication is sent to government depositories.

Census Catalog & Guide lists the numerous publications and statistical reports available from the U.S. Census Bureau, along with
ordering information. Further sources for government statistics
are also listed.

Federal Register and *Code of Federal Regulations* contain the regulations, proposed rules and notices written by Executive Branch
departments and agencies. The regulations are based on federal
laws or the President's executive order. The *Register* is published
five days a week; the *Code* compiles the *Register* into a multivolume, annual code book arranged by subject.

United States Code contains the full text of federal laws. The code
is arranged by subject, with recent code changes inserted into the
code books as "pocket parts." Periodically, new bound volumes
are issued.

Freedom of Information Act

Once upon a time, not all records compiled by the federal government
were public, and a vocal segment of the public, mainly journalists,
academics and citizen activists, grumbled rather loudly that keeping
records closed to public scrutiny had more to do with the personal
and political agendas of politicians and bureaucrats than with national
security or the confidentiality of people named in such documents. The
public has a right to know—Americans live in a democracy—these
critics pointed out.

The government still keeps secrets, but far fewer of them thanks to
enactment of the Freedom of Information Act (FOIA) in 1966. Now
the federal government must show the need for secrecy rather than
members of the public having to prove their right to the information;
now, that right is assumed. Agencies that deny access to records must
state their reasons. They may still keep information classified for reasons of national defense, foreign policy, trade secrets, agency personnel
matters, certain internal government correspondence or criminal inves-
tigations.

A companion to the FOIA, the Privacy Act of 1974, allows most
people to obtain the government files of which they're the subject and
restricts the release of personally identifiable federal information to
others.

The FOIA and Privacy Act also establish procedures for obtaining government documents and an appeal process, including a court challenge, for those denied access. The laws are not identical, however—some information denied under one law may be obtainable under the other, so cite both laws when requesting information pertaining to yourself; otherwise, cite only the FOIA.

The FOIA applies only to the Executive Branch, which includes cabinet departments, the U.S. military, independent regulatory agencies and corporations owned or controlled by the federal government. It does not apply to elected officials, including the president, the federal judiciary or those who receive federal grants or loans. Other public disclosure laws pertain to the president, vice president and Congress. The Presidential Records Act of 1978, for example, makes many documents of former presidents available under the FOIA, and most official proceedings of Congress are published in the *Congressional Record*.

The FOIA does not apply to Executive Branch information already subject to public disclosure, such as regulations published in the *Federal Register*. So first try other means to obtain the government documents you need before resorting to the FOIA, because the right to access government documents through FOIA doesn't necessarily mean that the procedures to obtain them are easy. As you no doubt already know, nothing is easy when it comes to the federal government.

First, you must know which federal agency has the information you want, because there's no central source through which to make your request. You can request FOIA information from more than one agency at a time, so if you're uncertain which agency has the information you need, just take a shot at a few of the most likely suspects. You can find a complete list of government agencies in the *United States Government Manual*, which is available in many libraries.

Second, information and records are not the same thing. Under the FOIA, you may only request records, i.e., documents, although not all documents are records. Agency employees' notes, for example, may be considered personal, not agency records. The FOIA does not define "record."

Third, you must describe a record specifically enough for an agency employee familiar with the general subject area to find the record in a reasonable amount of time. Some agencies are more helpful than others. Some may help you identify the specific records that contain the information you want, while others restrict their cooperation to taking down the title and date of the document or documents you want and then searching for them. Some may consider a request reasonably descriptive while others may reject it as vague, often because they store and index information differently. The Federal Bureau of Investigation, for instance, can easily search for records about an individual thanks to its central name index, while agencies without such a record-keeping device may find such a request too difficult to fulfill.

Although requesting a document by date and title will yield the best and quickest results, most people probably don't know the exact document they need, and fortunately it's not always necessary. In your request letter, explain the information you need as clearly and precisely as possible, though broadly enough to include everything you want.

For example, if you want to find out if there are any toxic waste dumps near your home, you're better off asking for records listing such dumps in your city, county or state. Asking for records containing the names of all toxic waste dumps in the country is overkill, and could cost you a bundle in fees, while a request for the names of toxic dumps within a two-mile radius of your address is too specific, and probably no such record containing that information exists. Include in your letter the exact information you want; it might clue agency employees to the most useful records.

Make your request in writing to the agency head or the agency's FOIA officer. State in the first sentence that you are making your request under the Freedom of Information Act, 5 U.S.C. Sec. 552, and/or the Privacy Act. Then state the document or documents you want along with the exact information you need. Next, ask for fee information or a fee waiver (explained in more detail below). At the bottom of the letter sign your name and write your name and address. It's a good idea to include your telephone number so agency employees can quickly clear up any misunderstandings. Write "Freedom of Information Act Request" in the bottom, left-hand corner of the envelope.

Components of large agencies such as the State Department may each have additional FOIA regulations, so it's best to check the regulations before making a request, although the simple procedures outlined here will meet minimum FOIA requirements. You can obtain a copy of specific FOIA regulations directly from the agency or in the *Code of Federal Regulations*, also available in many libraries.

Agencies cannot withhold an entire document just because some part of it contains classified information. They must release the document with the classified information blotted out. Agencies may deem some documents entirely classified. If you believe an agency is unwarranted in deleting certain items, you can appeal those items and the agency must justify in writing each deletion.

Just what constitutes classified information is a continual debate between researchers and the government, points out Gerard Colby, who authored with Charlotte Dennett *Thy Will Be Done—The Conquest of the Amazon: Nelson Rockefeller and Evangelism in the Age of Oil*, published by HarperCollins.

"FOIA is a process," says Colby. "It's up to researchers to find and then ask for documents, and then agency bureaucrats will review them."

"You're talking about covert actions in some of these cases," explains Dennett, "so when the covert action was happening, the action was classified information. But as time passes, the national security imperatives are removed or lessened."

Using FOIA, Colby and Dennett obtained documents showing that in the 1960s the U.S. government secretly supplied military equipment to the Colombian government for a counterinsurgency program despite a U.S. law prohibiting the use of U.S. military equipment for internal conflicts abroad.

Colby and Dennett first found documents indicating the weapons program at the Eisenhower presidential library. Portions of some documents were blacked out while other documents were either completely or partially removed. Cards or slips of paper were inserted in the files in place of the removed documents. With the help of the library staff, who are employees of the National Archives, they were able to sufficiently identify the documents and obtain the deleted information.

Under the law, an agency must respond to an FOIA request within ten working days, but don't hold your breath. Within about two weeks you'll probably receive a form letter informing you that your request has been placed at the end of a long line of requests. Agencies such as the FBI and CIA can take months to fulfill a request. Agencies also must respond to an administrative appeal within twenty working days. If either deadline is not met, individuals can then turn to the federal courts, which usually allow agencies extra time if they've demonstrated due diligence. The Privacy Act sets no time limit on an agency's response to a request nor does it provide for an administrative appeal, which is why you should cite both the FOIA and Privacy Act when seeking records about yourself.

Colby recommends writing your FOIA request on the stationery of a law firm if possible, and better yet, a Washington, DC, law firm familiar with the FOIA, to get the attention of agency officials and let them know you are serious about pursuing the information you want.

"If they don't want to release documents," says Colby, "sometimes they will delay and delay and delay. How you posture yourself is very important to make sure the review officer understands that you intend to go as far as necessary to force them to perform according to the law."

The government usually charges journalists, educators and private individuals only for document reproduction. People experienced in requesting FOIA records frequently ask in their request letters that they be notified if the charges exceed a fixed amount. That way they can change or withdraw their request, or request a waiver or fee reduction. Agencies must waive or reduce fees if you can convince them that the information you want significantly contributes to public understanding of government activities and is not for commercial purposes (the pitiful sum you'll be paid for your article is not considered commercial). Some agencies use fees as a way to discourage FOIA requests. Do not be deterred. Reargue your case for waived or reduced fees with a demand for a full explanation of the fee sum along with an itemized bill. FOIA allows for judicial appeal of fees.

For further help with FOIA requests, contact the FOIA Service Center, operated by the Reporters Committee for Freedom of the Press and the Society of Professional Journalists, Sigma Delta Chi, at 1735 I St., N.W., Washington, DC 20006; telephone: (202) 466-6312; or the Freedom of Information Clearinghouse, a project of Ralph Nader's Center for the Study of Responsive Law, at P.O. Box 19367, Washington, DC 20036; telephone: (202) 833-3000.

A couple of last reminders: Keep copies of your original request letter and all correspondence, including envelopes with postmarks, and make notes of all conversations with agency personnel, including the person's first and last name, position and the time and date of the conversation. You do all that anyway, don't you?

CHAPTER SIX

Online Research

Knowledge is power.—Francis Bacon

Learning without thought is labor lost.—Confucius

The term, Information Superhighway, has become such a cliche that even the most ardent cyberspace joyrider must be sick of hearing it. As clichéd as the name is, the highway itself is here to stay. And a good thing, too, for nonfiction writers, because the Information Superhighway is an incredibly powerful tool for gathering information. So whether you putt in the I-Highway slow lane, are still trying to find the on-ramp, or just wish the whole thing would collapse from hype and then we could return to that lovely, tree-lined avenue of information gathering, the sooner you learn how to negotiate the Information Superhighway the better.

There is one piece of good news about getting on the Information Superhighway: Learning to drive is getting easier and easier. It's analogous to learning how to use personal computers. When personal computers first came on the mass market in the 1970s, you had to be a certified nerd to use one. But now normal people use them without giving it a second thought, thanks to those nerds who have made computers simpler to use.

This chapter primarily will give you an idea of the vast resources available in cyberspace and how to access them. Much electronic information is the same as information you'd find in libraries or government offices, but accessible in different ways. Additionally, online discussion groups, which comprise a huge territory in cyberspace, can prove a rich source of information and interview subjects.

The big advantage to online research is that the information is usually much easier to access than at libraries and offices. It's available literally at your fingertips as your fingers glide along your computer keyboard or point and click your mouse. It's available, for the most part, whenever you want it, not just during business hours. And most important, you can access much more information than what's available at your local library. Library catalogs and other databases all over the world are at your beck and call.

Despite the advantages of online research, all is not a smooth ride. You might at times find yourself bewildered and frustrated as you plow through menu after menu of multiple-choice options leading to ever narrower categories of information resources. Persevere and you will reach the information you need.

Like the document research section of this book, I've leaned heavily on basic resources that lead you to other resources for getting information; there's simply too much information in cyberspace to encompass it all even in a book, let alone a chapter in a book. You will learn, however, where to go to get much of the information you'll need for most nonfiction research. I've also evaluated resources, mindful of the limited budget within which most freelance magazine writers must live. On the Information Superhighway, knowledge is not only power, it can cost a powerful lot of money, too.

This chapter is not a technical how-to manual. Whole books have been written about the technical end of using the Information Superhighway. The technology is different depending on the means by which you access it, and as I've just mentioned the technology is changing constantly, for the better.

Lay of the Land

For the complete neophyte, the following is a brief orientation tour along the Information Superhighway, what the Information Superhighway is and is not, and a few of the main roadside attractions.

The Information Superhighway, a phrase made popular by cyber-booster Al Gore, is not synonymous with the Internet, although the Internet is part of the Information Superhighway. Online devotees will lecture you vociferously should you dare make so egregious a mistake as to use the terms interchangeably. The Information Superhighway is basically the overarching term for the universe of computerized telecommunications, used to signify media such as interactive television, in which viewers make rudimentary responses to what they see on their TV screens; computer networks; or good old-fashioned voice communication, the connections of which are now largely computer controlled, along with other elements such as voice mail.

The Internet is the computer network portion of the Information Superhighway, and then only a part of all computer networking, albeit the largest single part. The name is aptly descriptive, because the Internet, or "Net" for short, is a true network of computers. Visualizing it as a net will help you understand how it works.

Originally developed by the U.S. defense establishment and later expanded to universities and scientific research institutions, the Internet now includes online computer users of all stripes for purposes as diverse as shopping, gathering research information, looking for jobs, looking for love, political organizing and sharing information on everything from recipes to vacation hideaways. The forms of information available on the Net have expanded from text to sound, graphics, and both still and moving pictures.

Often using their own computers at home, millions of people connect to the Internet through one-and-a-half-million host computers worldwide according to the Merit Net Information Center, a National Sciences Foundation-funded program to promote Internet activity. Host computers are the network nodes through which Net information travels. Host computers are usually located at universities, businesses, government agencies, private organizations and commercial online services. They are also known as Internet service (or access) providers. (A small percentage of individual Internet users have their own direct connection.)

Those same online devotees, who in another life were probably clerics arguing endlessly about how many angels can dance on the head of a pin, insist that the Internet is the connection between the network host computers. So if you operate solely within a host, which in itself can be quite large—like CompuServe, with more than three million subscribers—then according to the nitpickers, you are not yet out on the Net. But if you belong to CompuServe and send an electronic message to someone at Harvard, then you've traversed the Net because your message traveled between nodes. Don't worry about this fine point; it's a distinction without much practical difference.

Online computer research takes place through the Internet at sites located at host computers. Many universities, government agencies and nonprofit organizations make much of their information available for free. Commercial online services and commercial data banks charge for all or part of the information they store and the services they offer.

Briefly discussed below are the Internet's major components, so you'll better understand where and how to access the specific resources listed later in the chapter, and where and how to find your own resources.

Basic Net Building Blocks

The following major components of the Internet share similar purposes or operating environments. So, for instance, you might access information from a university or government computer by dialing directly with your modem, in which case your access method fits the bulletin board mode. The same university or government agency might also have a World Wide Web site, which you reach through an "http" address, and once at the site you can see and access the information in a different form. The Net blurs the distinction between what and how. Entities such as gopher and the World Wide Web, both of which are discussed later in this chapter, can be conceptualized as both a place where information resides and a method for finding information.

Commercial Online Services

While it's possible to access the Internet through your local university, library or local community Internet connection for free, many people access the Internet by way of commercial online services. Depending on which online service you subscribe to, you can access some or nearly all of the Internet's provinces and procedures, such as Usenet, World Wide Web, e-mail, gopher, ftp and Telnet. The old saw, you get what you pay for, was never truer than when it comes to online access. First, the commercial services build into their systems the software that makes it easy for you to navigate the Net, whereas free nets usually operate with systems much more daunting to learn, such as Unix. Second, commercial services offer information and services often not available on free nets, such as newspaper and magazine databases, news wire services and reference sources such as encyclopedias.

The major commercial services in the U.S. as of this writing are CompuServe, America Online, Prodigy and the relatively new Microsoft Network. The commercial services offer the widest range of services and, accordingly, are the most expensive, especially when you figure in the extra cost for premium services such as access to certain databases. Discussion groups, also known as forums or conferences and similar to Usenet news groups (discussed below), constitute the core of their service.

CompuServe and America Online also offer one of the least expensive ways to access newspaper and magazine index databases online. They also offer the full texts of newspaper and magazine articles, which is especially valuable to nonfiction researchers. CompuServe's Knowledge Index is especially praised by journalists experienced in online research. Such databases don't exist at Internet sites that provide free access because magazine and newspaper stories are "value-added," proprietary information for which people will pay a price. That's a real pain, since practically the first place a nonfiction writer looks for information about a subject is in previously published articles. Commercial data banks provide the best online magazine and newspaper databases, but they charge substantially higher prices.

Delphi, NetCom and The Pipeline specialize in Internet connections. They tend to cost less and offer fewer services. They provide essentially no newspaper and magazine databases, although access to daily news wire dispatches are available. If you're going to spend much time "surfing the net," as the saying goes, and can't afford to run up large bills, these services deserve serious consideration. Delphi has traditionally provided the most extensive Internet services, both in ease of use and search tools, although this is rapidly changing as the larger services race to catch up.

One other service worth mentioning is The WELL, which stands for Whole Earth 'Lectronic Link and was founded by Stewart Brand, founder of the Whole Earth Catalog. The WELL is often referred to as a "boutique" service because its approximately ten thousand members means it is relatively small for an online service. But it draws a disproportionate number of journalists and writers for its size. Its chat groups, called conferences, are cited by Net cognoscenti as having a notably high caliber of discussion as compared with the notably low caliber of discussion in some other Net neighborhoods. Another boutique service that draws a fair number of writers is ECHO, East Coast Hang Out.

Many online computer enthusiasts are content to stay in the womb of their online service and never venture onto the Internet, save for the occasional exchange of electronic mail with someone at a different site. Big online services such as CompuServe and America Online are virtual worlds unto themselves, and you could spend a lot of time exploring them. Also, online services provide a secure, comfortable environment for novice cybernauts. You can zip around within them with ease once you've learned their navigation procedures. If you venture beyond, however, you will have to learn what may at first seem like a dizzying array of additional terms and commands, not only to navigate the Internet itself but also to navigate within other nodes, say the Library of Congress. Things can get confusing and frustrating. But you'll find your comfort level quickly increases after only a few familiarization trips into cyberspace.

Although the databases of the large commercial services will satisfy basic journalistic research requirements, nonfiction writers with a serious need to collect information must move out of their cyberwombs and onto the Internet. The data contained in the computers of universities, organizations and government agencies, combined with the electronic networking of millions of people, provide a mind-boggling amount of free information. That's the abundance of information you want to get at, and what makes the Net so valuable to the nonfiction writer.

E-mail

One of the most popular features on the Internet is e-mail, which stands for, simply enough, "electronic mail." It's usually one-to-one communication. I send a note or memo to you at your e-mail address; you send back a response to mine. The advantages of e-mail are tremendous as compared to what Net cognoscenti snootily refer to as "snail mail," otherwise known as mail sent through the postal service. E-mail travels anywhere in the world at the speed of a telephone call, because, remember, all Internet communications take place over telephone lines. E-mail messages between sites are sometimes bundled together before being sent, but even then the delay is usually minutes or, on rare occasions, a few hours. E-mail to some foreign countries is also usually more reliable than sending mail by post, which often has a way of arriving weeks or months later, if at all. The cost compared to a long-distance fax or voice telephone call is cheaper since most subscribers to online services dial up their service providers toll free.

E-mail is a research tool in the same way as the telephone or the postal service is: You can send and receive information, set up interview appointments and even conduct interviews by e-mail. Interviewing by e-mail can be tricky. Many journalists feel uncomfortable finding an interview subject by e-mail and then conducting an interview by e-mail without having any other kind of connection. Many people assume other identities when traveling in cyberspace, because it's so easy. No one can see you or even hear your voice; they have only your words to rely on. A lot of journalists who use the Internet like the ease and convenience of finding interview subjects on the Net but when possible conduct the interview in person or by telephone. At least *hearing* the interview subject provides additional information and can help the perceptive journalist decide whether interview subjects are telling the truth and are in fact who they say they are.

But passing up the e-mail interview and relying on the telephone may be nothing more than an exercise in false security. Determined liars can lie as proficiently on the phone as they can by e-mail. The conscientious nonfiction writer needs to check out every interview subject's identity and story, no matter how it's obtained.

E-mail interviews can yield different results than telephone or in-person interviews since an e-mail interview is ultimately a written exchange of questions and answers. It is necessarily more static than the more protean interviews conducted in "live" interviews. On the other hand, e-mail responses can be more thoughtful and articulate than the spontaneous responses of a conventional interview.

Usenet

Usenet comprises a vast territory on the Internet; it is the collective name for the thousands of chat groups (more than four thousand and counting) that exist in cyberspace. Next to e-mail, Usenet is widely considered the most heavily used feature on the Internet. Usenet news groups, as they are called, are similar to chat groups within online services except you can only access them through the Internet. Usenet news groups belong to no one online service but rather are meeting places for members of many online services.

The name, news group, is a misnomer. No one commits formal journalism on Usenet, so don't look for AP dispatches or *Vanity Fair* celebrity profiles. All the news comes from news group participants, and in most groups it's unusual to see extended commentary or anything resembling an article. The basic format is statement and response, or "posts," in Net lingo. Someone posts a statement or question, and if he or she is lucky, someone responds. Some posts generate no responses; others spark lively, and at times heated, debate. Debate frequently gets so heated that Netheads use the word "flame" as a verb to describe the vituperative responses some posts provoke.

Here's a real-life example of a news group: Through my Internet service provider, Delphi, I connect to the rec.backcountry news group. A message reads, "2,143 messages have been posted in the last 14 days." I hit the "return" key, and the first full screen of rec.backcountry appears. A message at the top reads, "page 1 of 33. 2,143 messages in 626 discussion threads." The thirty-three pages, or screens, list the titles of the 626 discussion threads, which are simply the separate topics of discussion within the news group and which altogether contain 2,143 messages, or posts. The topics include discussions on subjects such as backpacking equipment, trail conditions and how to handle encounters with bears. I type in the number corresponding to a specific discussion thread, hit "return," and then I read the post and any posts in response to the original post. Newly posted topics are added to the end of the list and all the others move up a notch. After a set amount of time, usually a couple of weeks, a discussion thread scrolls into oblivion to ensure that the news group stays manageable (who wants to scroll through hundreds of pages of topic titles posted since the news group began?).

A Wealth of Sources

So what good is Usenet to you, the nonfiction writer? Plenty good, especially as a source for article ideas, contacts and interview subjects. You can find just about any interest group under the sun, from aeronautics students to fans of the humor writer P.G. Wodehouse, from multiple sclerosis sufferers to roller coaster enthusiasts. Along with the frivolous, much serious discussion and social activism takes place in some Usenet news groups. Everyone from environmentalists to school prayer advocates network through Usenet news groups. Internet access providers often provide a Usenet search service, or you can check printed Internet directories (a few of which are listed later in the chapter).

By tapping into news groups, journalists can find a readily obtainable pool of interview subjects. In doing research for this book, I posted a notice on alt.journalism asking about Internet sites that journalists found particularly useful. A few people replied directly in the topic, or thread, that I created with my post, but most of the dozen or so responses came by e-mail. I had previously obtained some sites mentioned through other sources, in published articles for instance, but one response led me to ProfNet, a free service through which academic experts will answer journalists' questions. Also, some responses gave me additional insight into the strengths and weaknesses of various Internet directories.

Identifying News Groups

You identify news groups by names that are composed of a series of usually two to four descriptive words separated mostly by dots and occasionally a dash or single underline keystroke that connects, say, a first and last name; like other Internet addresses, there are no spaces in news group names and no period at the end. Reading from the left, the names progress from the general to the specific, and are referred to as hierarchies.

Usenet news groups are first divided into broad subject categories: "rec" for recreation, "sci" for science and "alt" for alternative, among several categories. The next word narrows the category further, and the third (and usually last) word tells you specifically what the group is about. So in the "alt.fan" hierarchy you'll find alt.fan.bill-gates, a chat group for fans (and detractors) of computer software mogul Bill Gates. And in soc.culture you'll find groups on Italy, France, India, Singapore, Hong Kong and Argentina, among dozens of other nationalities. The alt.journalism hierarchy also includes several other news groups, including alt.journalism.print and alt.journalism.gay-press.

Groups in categories other than the "alt" category are usually better established and more sedate. "Alt" contains the far side of Net chat; here is where you'll find the cultural edge, in groups such as alt.pagans.magick and alt.society.anarchy.

Online services vary in the number of Usenet news groups they carry. So what you see in your online service's directory of Usenet groups is not necessarily all there is. Also check the news groups *news.groups*, *news.lists* and *news.announce.newgroups* for information on Usenet news groups, or look for news groups in printed directories or in directories on disks that are often included with how-to books about the Internet.

Bulletin Boards

Technically, every online site to which you can modem directly or telnet from your service provider is a bulletin board system, commonly abbreviated to BBS. Although some bulletin boards, such as government agency BBSs, are set up primarily to dispense information, it's most useful to think of bulletin boards as freestanding, special interest discussion groups similar to Usenet news groups or the chat groups on large commercial services.

In some ways, single-issue, discussion-oriented BBSs, of which there are an estimated forty-five thousand, are mavericks in cyberspace. They rise and fall at the whim of their "sysops," or system operators, and they are freestanding because they are mostly closed networks, that is, they are not connected with other Internet computer nodes. Even Usenet news groups are brought together under the Usenet rubric and various classifying hierarchies, and you must connect to them through the Internet, not by dialing directly. Bulletin boards are often limited in the numbers and geographic dispersal of their participants. Computer publications serving specific cities or regions may carry a directory of local BBSs. People banded together for a specific purpose and who want to keep a very low profile often communicate online through bulletin boards.

Mailing Lists

Mailing lists, also called listservs, are hybrids of e-mail and Usenet. Essentially, a mailing list is e-mail sent from one source to everyone on the list. It works something like direct mail, except the people sending you the information are usually trying to sell you ideas not products, and you requested the information. Groups interested in everything from Indian culture to Christian fundamentalism operate mailing lists. Mailing lists are a great way to get a steady, often daily stream of information on a subject. In fact, many people find their e-mail boxes jammed as their mailing lists pump out information seemingly nonstop.

With some mailing lists, the information flows one way, from the organizing source. With others, list members may also post messages for everyone else on the list to read, in which case the mailing list takes on the character of a discussion group. To get on a list, you subscribe (almost always free of charge) by e-mailing your request to the list administrator. When subscribing, make sure to send your request to the administrator's e-mail address, not the mailing list address. Subscribing instructions, often available in directories, usually include a key phrase to write in the body of your e-mail request.

World Wide Web

The World Wide Web, or Web for short, represents the vanguard of Internet technology. As such, it indicates the future look of the Internet, and, no surprise, it is the hottest place to be on the Net. Why is the Web so hot? Two reasons: Information can be presented in an integrated, multimedia package of still pictures, moving pictures, sound and text; and the Web provides a relatively easy, powerful way to access that information. Everyone from traditional Internet players such as universities and government agencies to commercial businesses and individuals are rushing to create their own Web sites, also commonly referred to as home pages. (A home page is technically the initial, introductory information you see on your screen when you connect to a Web site. It's similar to a magazine's front cover and table of contents page combined.)

Conceptually speaking, the World Wide Web is both a place for information and a means for obtaining it. All Web sites look and operate the same way, but they look and operate differently than, say, Usenet news groups, which share their own look and operating characteristics. A software tool called hypertext is what creates the World Wide Web. Hypertext basically works like this: With your mouse, you click onto a highlighted word within a document, or use a numbered command if your computer lacks graphic capabilities, and a document with more information relating to the highlighted word appears on your screen. The new document usually belongs to the Web site to which you originally connected, but it may instead belong to a completely different Web site.

So, for example, you may connect to an online Web directory such as Yahoo, and when you find a site that interests you, you click your mouse and the next thing you know you're at that other site. Unfortunately, the increasing number of commercial enterprises that have set up Web sites to promote their wares tend not to create hypertext connections to other Web sites, which could very well be their competitors. Still, they can provide you with plenty of useful information. I gathered much of my information about the commercial data banks discussed next in this chapter by rummaging around on their Web sites.

It's really easy to get lost in the maze of hypertext connections. You jump from one document or Web site to another, and the next thing you know you can't figure out how to get back to the one with the most useful information. So before leaping ahead, note documents and Web sites you like. You also can usually set your communications program (that's the software that operates your modem) to "capture" an online session on your computer's hard drive. With a "capture" or "dump" file, you can go back and see where you've been on the Web.

Commercial Data Banks

With all that free information available on government and university computers and in discussion groups, why on earth would you would you pay a healthy fee to online data banks such as Lexis/Nexis and Dow Jones News/Retrieval?

There are some pretty good reasons, if the value in time saved and information gained is worth the cost. First, these data banks maintain dozens of databases containing the newspaper, magazine and journal articles, i.e., copyrighted information, that most nonfiction writers check as one of the first steps in researching a story. Few such free, article databases are available to the general public on the Net. (Books other than computer manuals are also generally not available on the Internet, except for uncopyrighted classics from Project Gutenberg.) Second, the information is timely and kept up-to-date. And third, it is organized so you can search in ways most familiar and useful to you, the researcher, by subject, title, author, publication or company, geographic area or any of various other ways you want to slice the information pie.

Online data banks also have a few important advantages over articles obtained in libraries. At a library, you first look through an index such as *Reader's Guide* or InfoTrac to find article titles that suggest the article might prove useful; then you look for the article on the shelves or on microfilm; then you copy it if you can use it. Depending on the data bank, you can search an index of titles, see an abstract of the article (InfoTrac also provides abstracts for many articles, but not all), quickly access the *full text* of the article for viewing on your computer screen, and then download the article if you want it.

In addition, online data banks often contain articles from many more publications than the average public library. Plus, you can perform online research from your own home and often at times most convenient to you. As you can see, online data bank research is a much more efficient way to gather information than traditional library research. No wonder many professional researchers such as journalists, academics and financial analysts swear by commercial, online data banks.

Unlike free Net resources, which almost invite you to dally in their databases, the cost to use commercial data banks will concentrate the mind considerably toward planning an effective search strategy. A typical search might cost anywhere from five to fifty dollars. Ask yourself exactly what you need the information for, how much of it you need, and what would be the best way of going about getting it. Ask yourself these questions before you log on and the clock starts ticking, and before you display or download every article you can find remotely pertaining to your subject and for which you'll likely pay by the page or article. Think about exactly how you want to phrase your keyword search and the commands you'll need to accomplish your search, and write them down if need be so you won't have to figure it out online when the clock is ticking.

To yield the best results quickest, you might avoid the temptation of beginning your search with full-text databases. Rather, start with databases of titles or titles and abstracts. Log off to examine the information you've gathered, then go back online to review and retrieve the full text. This two-step method saves a possibly prolonged search through full-text databases, which saves you time and money. A search of abstracts provides perhaps the best middle ground, since titles alone can often prove cryptic or misleading.

Although some data banks are making it easier to search their databases by allowing you to frame your search questions in plain English, many still maintain search procedures based on Boolean logic. Some data banks offer hands-on, introductory practice sessions at locations around the U.S. to help you learn their search methods, along with a couple of free hours online to fumble around if you sign up. Formal training in search techniques may make sense if you plan frequent visits to data banks, otherwise you may want to consider hiring an expert searcher through the Association of Independent Information Professionals at 245 Fifth Ave., Ste. 2103, New York, NY 10016; telephone: (212) 779-1855; e-mail: 73263.12@compuserve.com.

Listed below are a few of the better, and better-known, data banks that many journalists favor:

Dialog. Owned by Knight-Ridder, which also owns one of the U.S.'s largest newspaper chains, Dialog carries hundreds of databases on just about every imaginable topic. Its roots in serving government and university research laboratories makes it particularly strong in science and medicine; it carries Medline, a key source for reviewing medical journal abstracts. Dialog's Knowledge Index service gives you access to many Dialog databases during evenings and weekends at a cut-rate cost. Contact Dialog at Knight-Ridder Information Inc., 2440 El Camino Real, Mountain View, CA 94040; telephone: (800) 334-2564.

Lexis/Nexis. The twin Lexis/Nexis data banks are among the oldest and most extensive of the online data banks. (L)exis stands for "law," and (N)exis for "news." As of this writing, Nexis carries the only complete text of *The New York Times* online. Contact Lexis/Nexis at 9443 Springboro Pike, P.O. Box 933, Dayton, OH 45401; telephone: (800) 543-6862, or for Nexis only, (800) 346-9759.

Dow Jones News/Retrieval. Dow Jones Inc., publisher of the *Wall Street Journal*, is the giant of financial and economic news. As such, the Dow Jones News/Retrieval service is unparalleled in the amount of online business information it makes available, including not only news articles but also indices on stocks, bonds and other securities, and reports on companies. Contact Dow Jones News/Retrieval at P.O. Box 300, Princeton, NJ 08543-0300; telephone: (609) 452-1511.

NewsNet. NewsNet specializes in independent trade and industry newsletters, which often prove an excellent source for trends and insider information that might not surface in the general news media for weeks or months. NewsNet carries the leading newsletters in a broad range of areas. Contact NewsNet at 945 Haverford Ave., Bryn Mawr, PA 19010; telephone: (800) 345-1301.

CompuServe. Compared to other online conference services, CompuServe offers substantial research material, which is why I've listed it here. CompuServe's various databases will probably serve your basic research needs and are probably a good place to start. Magazine Database Plus and The Newspaper Library contain, respectively, dozens of major magazines and newspapers available for downloading. For serious searches—and for more money—CompuServe's IQuest provides access to several outside commercial data banks such as Dialog and NewsNet. Contact CompuServe at 5000 Arlington Center Blvd., Columbus, OH 43220; telephone: (800) 848-8199.

Net Navigators and Search Tools

With the millions of pieces of information in cyberspace—reports, indices, names and addresses—a couple of important questions arise: How do you find what you need and how do you get it once you find it? The following net navigators and search tools will help you accomplish your goals. While some people still use the ftp-Archie method of finding and obtaining electronic documents, gopher has largely supplanted it for reasons explained shortly, and the newest Net navigator, the World Wide Web, is mounting a strong challenge to gopher. When using the search tools described below, keep in mind an important point of Net etiquette, or netiquette: Whenever possible, connect to the remote computer geographically closest to your online service to cut down on an increasing problem, Net traffic jams.

Telnet

Telnet is a simple means by which you can connect from your home base on the Internet to another computer, commonly referred to as a remote computer or a host. So, rather than paying for a long distance phone call to connect directly to FedWorld from my home in California, I log on to my service provider, Delphi, which requires only a local phone call, and from Delphi I telnet to fedworld.gov. My home computer now behaves as a terminal of the FedWorld computer. This means I must negotiate my way through the system using the FedWorld commands, not the commands I use for Delphi or for my own home computer. But typical of remote computers providing telnet sessions, the menu-based options on the screen allow me to move about the system, so it's not much of a problem. A remote computer will also usually provide login instructions when you first connect. If no instructions are given, try "guest" or "newuser" at the "userid" prompt, or the user name you usually use. Any computer open to the public, such as electronic library catalogs, are usually accessible through telnet.

Ftp

Ftp, or file transfer protocol, allows you to retrieve, or download, information files from a remote computer directly to your own home computer or, alternatively, first to your personal home directory on your service provider's computer and then to your home computer. Ftp is also commonly called anonymous ftp because you usually type "anonymous" at the "userid" prompt ("ftp" may work instead); at the "password" prompt, type your electronic address. Once logged on to the remote site, you see directories with lists of file names. You cannot, however, actually enter the files to see whether the information is what you want. You must ascertain a file's content by its name, which is a bit hit-and-miss. By executing the proper commands, which includes identifying the file by name, you can then direct the computer to send you the entire file in either binary or ASCII formats.

OK, now that you know how to obtain a file, how do you find the file you need? The answer is Archie. Archie maintains a database of file names from host computers around the world, along with the names of those host computers and the directories and subdirectories in which the files reside. You telnet to your local Archie server computer—numerous Archie servers are scattered around the world—and perform a search of file names or file type by using a keyword. Archie then pinpoints the location of a file by its file name, directory and/or subdirectory, and host computer. You log off the Archie server, telnet or otherwise log on to the host computer, then download the file using anonymous ftp.

Gopher

A newer, easier way to get information through the Internet rather than using ftp and Archie is gopher. Like the World Wide Web, cybernauts conceive of gopher as both method and place; gopher is a software for seeking out information and the computers that provide gopher service are known as gopher servers or gopher sites, or just plain gophers. The information they collectively generate is known as gopherspace. More than fifteen million items of information from more than five thousand gopher servers are available to you in gopherspace. For its relative ease of use, gopher is one of the most powerful ways to gather information on the Internet.

With gopher, you log on to a gopher site through your Internet service provider and you are presented with a menu from which you choose one of several listed options. As you narrow your search with subsequent choices from a succession of menus, you eventually turn up the text of an actual document on your screen. If you want it, you download it.

Gopherspace illustrates the wonderful, tangled network that is the Internet. When you log on to a gopher site, you can search that gopher's database only, or you can use a search method called Veronica to look for the information you want on a database of gopher menus worldwide located on another computer, called a Veronica server, unless the gopher you're already logged on to is also a Veronica server. When you find what you want, the gopher you're logged on to will access the information of the remote gopher. In short, you can jump around the world from computer to computer in minutes searching for information.

Tunnel through gopherspace using subject-area menus if you're not exactly sure what you're looking for or if you just want to see what's out there. But for more focused searches try Veronica. You can perform two kinds of searches with Veronica: the titles of any kind of information in gopherspace, such as directory titles, document titles, World Wide Web site names, Usenet news group names, Internet addresses; or directory titles only. A search through all of gopherspace will usually yield more "hits" from scattered sources, possibly an overwhelming number of them if your search keyword is broad enough. Conversely, a directory search will yield fewer hits but will show you where in gopherspace the information you want is concentrated.

WAIS

With WAIS, which is short for Wide Area Information Servers, you search the individual databases of WAIS servers, but unlike Archie and Veronica, the keyword you type searches through the texts of the documents or files themselves, not merely file names or descriptive words in menus. Plus, WAIS uses a numerical scoring system to prioritize the list of file names that will turn up on your screen as a result of your search, based on the number of times your keyword or phrase turns up in the document. WAIS shows you a list of databases with a brief description of the topics to which they pertain. You choose a database and then perform your WAIS search. You access WAIS through a WAIS client. Your online service may provide a menu-based system, otherwise telnet to *quake.think.com* or *nnsc.nsf.net* and log in as "wais." Once you've found a database of related files, WAIS is a powerful tool for obtaining the files you need. WAIS will not only point you to text files, but to sound and pictures as well.

Net Addresses: What They Are, What They Mean

To the neophyte, an Internet address is often a long, incomprehensible assemblage of words, dots, slashes, numbers and abbreviations. There's no need to learn what an address means to use it, but as a source of information, it helps to know, just as knowing street addresses and telephone numbers can provide valuable information beyond simply how to contact a source. Fortunately, it's easy to figure out an Internet address if you learn a few basics.

First, an Internet address is commonly known as a URL, for Uniform Resource Locator. URL still most commonly refers to World Wide Web addresses, for which it was first used, but many people have begun referring to any Internet address as a URL.

Each piece of information in an Internet address is separated by a dot or sometimes a single slash. For e-mail, the "@" symbol separates an individual's name and his or her access provider, such as president@whitehouse.gov. As you can see from this fairly obvious example, Internet addresses start with the most specific information at the left and build increasingly to the general as you read to the right. It works similarly to a postal address, which usually proceeds from the specific to the general top to bottom when written on an envelope.

Sometimes addresses begin with the access method, say telnet, gopher, http or ftp, followed by a colon and two slashes, as in "gopher://gopher.lib.virginia.edu." Everything to the right of "gopher://" is the actual address. Depending on your Internet access provider and the type of Internet navigation software you use, you may or may not have to include the method name, colon and slashes when accessing a site.

The first piece of information in an Internet address is the individual person or computer site you want to reach, then the name, usually abbreviated, of the entity such as an online service or university, and last the category of entity. Addresses outside the U.S. also contain a country abbreviation at the end, such as "uk" for United Kingdom and "ca" for Canada. If the address is longer, the abbreviations in the middle usually refer to groups within groups, say a department within a university or an online project on an institution's large computer. You may occasionally see variations of this address format.

It's helpful to know the last section of the address, also known as the domain, since it tells you the kind of organization. The main abbreviations are as follow: "edu" for educational and research institutions; "gov" for government entities; "mil" for the U.S. military; "org" for organizations, usually nonprofit; "net" for computer network support centers; and "com" for businesses, including commercial online services.

As you may have already figured out from the two easy examples cited above, "president@whitehouse.gov" is the e-mail address for the President, at the White House, the federal government; and "gopher.lib.virginia.edu" is the address for the University of Virginia's library gopher.

Sometimes the very last bit of information supplied at the end is a number. It is the port to which you must connect at the computer represented by the Internet address.

As a computer user, you know you must give precisely the correct command to get your computer to do what you want it to do. It's the same when accessing nodes or e-mail addresses on the Internet. So take note: There are no dots at the end of Internet addresses. When you see an Internet address at the end of sentence in a book or an article, that dot is the period, not part of the Internet address.

Directories and Search Guides

The Internet's *raison d'être* is to make massive amounts of information available as easily as possible. It is both blessing and a curse. All that information, but how to find what you need? The Net itself is the answer: Use the Net to find information on the Net. Online search guides and directories provide many more listings of Internet sites than the ink-on-mashed-trees directories, and the listings are usually more up-to-date thanks to the ease with which online material can be updated. But especially for the novice cybernaut, books are a lot quicker and easier to use, and even experienced cybernauts sometimes look to books for ease of use. After all, with a book, all you have to do is open it and look in the index or flip to the alphabetized listing. That's a lot simpler than starting your computer, connecting to your online service, logging in, clicking to an online directory, then performing a keyword search.

Online Guides

Internet Information Listing. A comprehensive grab bag that includes a list of Internet providers, Internet guides, help files for ftp and telnet and access to many popular gophers.

> gopher://mindvox.phantom.com

Internet Services List or Yanoff List. An excellent, comprehensive list of Internet resources that contains hundreds of gopher and World Wide Web sites arranged in alphabetized, broad subject categories.

> ftp://csd4.csd.uwm.edu
> path: /pub/inet.services.txt

Internet Phone Books. A gopher that contains resources for finding e-mail addresses on the Internet, including Netfind, WHOIS and InterNIC. It also contains zip code information and a directory of international telephone area codes.

> gopher://cs4sun.cs.ttu.edu

CSORG, Clearinghouse for Subject-Oriented Internet Resource Guides. As the name denotes, subject-oriented guides are available from this gopher site.

gopher://una.hh.lib.umich.edu/11/inetdirs

EINet Galaxy. A comprehensive, global guide to Internet information and services, with more than 140,000 hyperlinked titles.

http://galaxy.einet.net/galaxy.html

http://www.einet.net

InterNIC Home Page. A National Science Foundation-sponsored project to make the Internet easier to use. The service provides information about using and finding resources on the Internet.

http://www.internic.net

Yahoo. One of the most popular World Wide Web guides. The guide provides a series of menus arranged by subject that eventually directly link you to Web sites on your subject.

http://www.yahoo.com

World Wide Web Worm. A comprehensive list of Web home page addresses and other URLs and ways to search the Web.

http://www.cs.colorado.edu/home/mcbryan/www.html

Hytelnet. A guide to library catalogs in the Americas and Europe; also lists Web, WAIS and gopher sites.

gopher://gophlib@gopher.yale.edu

ftp://ftp.usask.ca

Offline Directories (You Know, Books)

Especially for the Net novice, printed Internet directories are often quicker and easier to browse through, and far less intimidating, than using electronic, online directories. They may also cost less in the long run due to online connect fees. But compared to electronic directories, which are so easy to update, you'll find hard-copy directories somewhat out-of-date.

Internet Yellow Pages. Christine Maxwell, New Riders Publishing, Indianapolis, Indiana, categorizes site entries by title and subject keywords, includes a short description, sponsor name, audience information, contact and various methods of connecting to the sites (e-mail, telnet, gopher, WWW). More comprehensive than and not to be confused with the same title published by Osborne McGraw-Hill.

The Internet Directory. Eric Braun, Fawcett Columbine, New York, New York, categorizes alphabetically within Internet mode categories (ftp, gopher, Usenet), except also includes category on library catalogs. It contains many more listings than the *Internet Yellow Pages*, but it's weak on World Wide Web listings.

Using the World Wide Web. Bill Eager, Que Corporation, Indianapolis, Indiana, is a combination of how to use the World Wide Web and a listing of Web sites by subject.

Research Services

ProfNet. Short for Professors Network, ProfNet is a network of public information officers at some eight hundred institutions in seventeen countries that finds expert sources for journalists and authors. It represents universities, corporations, and government and nonprofit agencies focusing on scholarship and research. The service is free. Ask for a copy of ProfNet's instructions before making your first query.

e-mail: profnet@sunysb.edu.
telephone: (800) 776-3638
fax: (516) 689-1425

Net Research Resources

LOCIS, Library of Congress Information System. The Library of Congress catalog online.

telnet://locis.loc.gov

Yale Directory of Internet Libraries. A gopher site with as comprehensive a list as possible of international library catalogs accessible from the Internet and their subject strengths.

gopher://gophlib@gopher.yale.edu

National Library of Medicine Gopher. An online medical library database covering the NLM, which is sponsored by the World Health Organization and is considered the world's largest single-topic library.

> gopher://el-gopher.med.utah.edu
> gopher://gopher.who.ch

National Institute of Health Library Online Catalog. A catalog of books and journals in the NIH library, but not of individual journal articles.

> telnet://nih-library.ncrr.nih.gov

FedWorld. The gateway to the federal government online and the most centralized, online source for U.S. Government information. Through it you can access federal databases, news releases, transcripts of presidential speeches and press conferences, catalogs of government reports, and obtain the phone numbers of federal agency bulletin boards. You can also navigate between federal departments and agencies.

> telnet://fedworld.gov
> http://www.fedworld.gov
> telephone: (703) 321-8020

CHAPTER SEVEN

Interviews and Field Research

With reference to the narrative of events, far from permitting myself to derive it from the first source that came to hand, I did not even trust my own impressions, but it rests partly on what I saw myself, partly on what others saw for me, the accuracy of the report being always tried by the most severe and detailed tests possible.—Thucydides, fifth-century Greek historian

The most essential gift for a good writer is a built-in shockproof shit-detector.—Ernest Hemingway

D o all the library research you want, spend hours and hours trolling for information in cyberspace, but at some point you must do what many a reporter dreads: You must get out of the office and into the field.

The best nonfiction comes from original research, and more often than not the most exciting original research comes from the field. Even the best stories drawn exclusively from primary written sources are still the journalistic equivalent of leftovers. (Remember, "new" as in news stories.) You can find a consumer trend in a haystack of statistical reports, but if you don't go into the field to report on the people who bring that statistic to life—who they are, what they look like, how they behave, what they say about why they behave like they behave—then all you have is another report.

Fieldwork involves two aspects: observing people and places, and talking to people.

Interviews

Interviews are the lifeblood of articles, and quotes—people telling their own stories in their own words or commenting on someone's else's story—enliven articles. The reader snaps to attention when a quote appears in a story; something "live" is happening.

Broadly defined, an interview occurs anytime you, as a journalist, question someone to obtain information for a story, whether by talking to the person directly or through an exchange of written communications. An interview implies your intent to quote the interview subject in your story, but as we'll see, that's not always the case. An interview can last from ten seconds to ten months, or longer, though usually it refers to a single interviewing session. It yields everything from the print equivalent of a sound bite to a biographical full confession.

The dread that writers associate with field research most often pertains to conducting interviews. Standing back and playing the unobserved observer suits many writers' temperaments. If they do dread interviewing people, novice journalists and seasoned veterans often dread it for different reasons: Young reporters are afraid; old reporters are bored. Novices often feel they're being pushy when they ask someone for an interview and prying when asking questions. But that's the beauty of slipping into the role of journalist: You're licensed to pry and satisfy your curiosity; it's your job. You must nearly always pry politely and in the interest of your story, and at times gently and subtly, but pry you may, and indeed must, if you're going to get your story.

Kinds of Interviews

Interviews and quotes serve different purposes depending on the kind of story. Interviews and quotes also often serve different purposes in the same story. A personality profile usually requires that the primary interview involve the subject, and that the interview supply the lion's share of quotes. (On occasion, journalists will write profiles on uncooperative subjects, including dead ones, by talking to lots of people who know the subject, but they won't actually interview the subject.) Q&As, by definition, require extended quotes from the primary source or sources; they are edited records of one or more interviewing sessions. Articles consisting mainly of reported facts, say a typical summer service piece on preventing skin cancer, usually require only concise quotes from experts and maybe an average person with whom the reader can identify. The typical feature article on a social phenomenon or incident requires the gamut of interviews.

How to Get Interview Subjects

Unless you're shooting for Michael Jackson or the President of the United States as an interview subject, getting people to talk for publication is not all that hard. People want to talk; they want everyone to know their opinions; they want to bask in the spotlight. In our celebrity-obsessed society, everyone wants to be a celebrity. That's why there's no end of ordinary people who go on TV talk shows and subject themselves to verbal abuse and humiliation. Better to be the object of hateful attention than no attention at all. Even people who've had their share of the spotlight want more. It seems almost everyone is flattered when you ask their opinion.

There are a few different kinds of interview subjects, corresponding to, as mentioned above, the kind of story you're doing and how the subjects fit into the story. There are the central players, the ones who move the action along or who are acted upon, and for these people you want in-depth interviews that reveal primarily their personalities and motivations, and secondarily factual information. If you've conceived a story and done some preliminary research, then you've probably already stumbled upon these people, since you'd have no story without them.

But sometimes you hear or read about a social phenomenon and need a subject to illustrate it. You don't want to use some other writer's example in an article you've read, but the article might suggest other interview subjects. If you can access the Internet, look for interview subjects among the thousands of chat groups online. Solicit for interview subjects by placing a classified ad or write a letter to the editor of a newspaper read by potential interview subjects. Also talk to specialists and experts. Let's say you want to talk to families dealing with Alzheimer's disease but don't know any. Contact social workers who work with Alzheimer's families at a hospital, clinic or public health department. They probably won't be able to hand over the names and telephone numbers of their clients, but more often than not they'll willingly serve as intermediaries, especially if you ask to interview the social workers for your story.

Expert Subjects

It's pretty easy to find experts. You'll run across experts quoted in books and articles related to your subject. Experts often write their own books and articles, so you can quite possibly interview someone whose book you're using as a resource. To find experts in academia, look up relevant journal articles or call university departments and ask for the professor who specializes in your subject of inquiry. A word of advice when dealing with academics: Academics often prefer talking with journalists who want an in-depth understanding of a subject rather than serving, as they see it, as a quote machine or fact dispenser for a superficial, journalistic treatment of a subject to which they may have devoted their entire careers.

An excellent reference book for finding experts in the U.S. is *Who Knows What: The Essential Business Resource Book*, by Daniel Starer, published by Henry Holt and Company. Written expressly for journalists, this 1,200-plus-page book contains more than five hundred subject categories, each with about a half-dozen or so total listings under the categories of associations, periodicals, libraries, companies and federal government agencies (state government offices are listed in state subject headings).

As mentioned in chapter five, associations are also excellent sources for finding experts, and often nonexpert interview subjects as well. Check the *Encyclopedia of Associations*. When you call, ask immediately to speak with the public relations department (sometimes under marketing); PR people are familiar with writers' needs. On occasion, you may want to avoid the PR people. If your questions appear detrimental to the organization, PR people will run interference for their bosses, which is also part of their job.

Also check government office directories such as the *United States Government Manual* for leads to government experts. The *Washington Information Directory*, published by Congressional Quarterly, lists useful government and nongovernment contacts in Washington, including names, addresses and telephone numbers.

Subjects as Commentators

As indicated, experts are often commentators on the players' actions. Nonexpert commentators include friends, family, colleagues and coworkers, acquaintances and almost anyone who's had anything to do with the subject and has something pertinent to say. Interview subjects are like links in a chain; one leads to another. Keep asking, "Who else can I talk to?" or "Who knows about that?" and most of the time you'll find plenty of people to interview.

Most writers make first contact by telephone, but letter, fax, e-mail, telegram or a combination of two or all five is also acceptable. If a potential interview subject refuses an interview request during your initial telephone call to set a time, follow up with a letter making the case for why an interview would be in the person's best interest—then follow up on your letter with another telephone call. Be persistent.

Public figures especially want to know what's in it for them. A story that promotes them, their business, product or point of view is a persuasive argument. So, too, is the argument that they'll want to respond to their critics, whom you will quote even if they refuse to cooperate. Explain that you want to be fair and tell their side of the story.

Most public figures are savvy enough to know already what's in an interview for them; they don't need your advice. But if they are reluctant or refuse, make the case with finesse and be polite. After all, you approached them; you're the one asking for something, even if they'll get something in return. Rare is the situation when rudeness is a better tactic than politeness. Being polite doesn't mean being timid or apologetic for requesting the interview, however. Exude confidence—but not arrogance—even if you're apprehensive.

When approaching an interview subject, immediately identify yourself and explain as concisely as possible what you want. This is the opening of what you might think of as a preinterview interview: "Hi, I'm C. Smith and I'm doing a story on UFOs for *Fanciful Flights* magazine. We're looking at how people's lives have been affected by encounters with extra-planetary beings. Sue T. at the Close Encounters Association told me you'd spent some time aboard the *SS Alien*. I'd like to talk with you about your experience."

Notice the low-key approach. Interview subjects, especially inexperienced ones, can get skittish even if they do desire to talk; no need to scare them off with a declarative sentence involving the word "interview." "Interview" connotes a formality and importance that might intimidate the subject. Make it sound like a friendly chat. You can use a more direct approach with professional interviewees.

Briefly explaining the focus of your story helps interview subjects better understand exactly what you want from them, and it invites a sense of shared purpose. It also reassures them that you mean no harm. If you do mean harm—and that can be a legitimate journalistic endeavor—then be vague about your story to suggest an innocent intention. Journalists do lie on occasion about their stories and even their identities, but only in extraordinary situations, when by revealing their true identity and purpose they may put themselves in physical danger or make it necessarily impossible to obtain critical information regarding illegal activities. Identifying the person or source who referred you reassures the subjects that there's some familiar, legitimate connection between you, a total stranger, and them.

You might be asking, but what if I don't have an assignment for my story, like C. Smith? C. Smith never mentioned anything about an assignment. It's a sneaky, semantical fast shuffle, and best to be avoided. If you have an assignment, then say it: "I'm doing a story on assignment for *Fanciful Flights* magazine about UFOs." If you've received no commitment from a magazine but the editors have written or told you that they're willing to review the completed manuscript on speculation, and if you still want to pursue the story under those conditions, then go ahead and say, "*Fanciful Flights* magazine is interested in a story about UFOs." You also don't have to say you're doing it for anyone. True, an assignment from a nationally recognized magazine opens doors faster than no assignment. But remember, most people, especially those who are never asked their opinion for publication, are only too happy to be interviewed.

Quickly follow up your opening pitch with an estimate of how much time you'll need for the interview and where you'd like to conduct it. If the interview subject is a busy person, emphasize that you'll take as little time as possible. You can slightly underestimate the amount of time you think you'll actually need. Once in the door, you usually can extend your time a bit.

Suggest the place for the interview as suits your needs, at their home, office, by telephone. Suggest a place that will help reveal your subject's character and in which your subject will feel most comfortable to reveal to you their intimate thoughts, feelings and details of their lives, if your objective is to capture the essence of a person. Usually, you'll only get one interviewing session, so carefully decide what you want from the interview and how it fits into your story.

Unfortunately, sometimes one setting precludes an interview subject from feeling both comfortable and in the best representative environment for your story. For example, perhaps you're interviewing a high-powered advertising executive. At the office, you may get a chance to see how the person interacts with colleagues in pressured situations, and you can describe the work environment in your article. On the other hand, you're likely to get more personal information if you get the person away from the office, say at home, at a restaurant or during a leisure activity, say horseback riding. It all depends on what you're after. If you have the time, you can place the subject in varying environments for better effect (see the example below of Laura Hagar's interview with Richard Ofshe).

For short interviews, which usually means interviews in which you want a few observations or an expert comment, the telephone works fine. Obviously your own time and resources come into play. Try to make the time of the interview convenient for the interview subject.

And last—and this is important—be prepared to begin an initial interview upon first contact, pen in hand or fingers on the keyboard. People often blurt out a few spontaneous comments that go right to the heart of the matter, and those comments are often the best quotes you'll get.

Preparing and Planning the Interview

Before you make first contact with an interview subject to set up the interview, you've no doubt already done some preliminary research. But in the best cases, that's not nearly enough when it comes to the interview itself. Enter the interview stuffed with facts about your subject if that subject is the focus of your story. For brief interviews, such background research is unnecessary, although whatever background you can get about a subject is helpful when interviewing an expert, as well as knowing at least the expert's basic bio. Why insult the person with total ignorance? You must at least know the reason for your interview. Despite the work habits of famous nonfiction writer John McPhee, who reportedly shuns preinterview research, almost all other writers benefit enormously from knowing almost everything there is to know about primary interview subjects before sitting down and actually interviewing them.

Benefits of Preinterview Research

1. *You can ask more intelligent questions and dig deeper into your subject's character.* This presumes there's a written record on your subject, which there probably is if your subject is already notable in any way. Use previously published facts as a springboard to delve deeper into your subject or to take the story in the direction you want to go. There's no better way to annoy a busy, public person than to cover ground trod many times over in previous interviews. Indeed, the whole point of your story should be to break new ground.

2. *You can make more effective use of your interview time.* High-powered, newsworthy people are typically short on time and will not sit still for time-consuming interviews, so you have to make every minute count. In addition, you can quickly zero in on getting answers to the focus of your story.

3. *You can learn in a background check about any pitfalls to avoid during the interview and about your subject's likely reactions to certain questions.* This will help you chart the course of the interview and anticipate how to handle the rough moments you may encounter when asking tough questions.

4. *You can more effectively gauge whether your interview subject is lying, dissembling, prevaricating or otherwise trying to mislead you.* People conceal or pretty-up the truth with alarming regularity, especially for public consumption; that's why the term "spin control" has entered the popular lexicon.

Almost everyone wants to show themselves in their best light—we all do it almost all the time—but professional interviewees are particularly adept at it. Though it's a harsh judgment, the word "politician" is often synonymous with "liar," and entertainment celebrities especially are keenly aware of their myth-making duties. Not all of us naturally possess that highly developed, built-in shit detector Hemingway talked about—we naturally want to believe people—so getting the low-down on your interview subjects before the interview helps you control their spin.

Plotting Your Interview Strategy

If there's no written or broadcast record of your interview subjects, you can still find out something about them. Talk to their friends, families, associates, whomever. Delve into the subject's childhood, depending on how much it would improve the story as weighed against time and resource limitations. Many nonfiction writers, in fact, employ this same preparatory interviewing strategy when it comes to stories about people who have compiled lengthy public records. As famous muckraker Jessica Mitford advises, "Absorb all available information about your subject before approaching the target of the investigation."

Once you've prepared for the interview with background research, map out your interview strategy. Planning the interview forces you to understand the focus of your story and how the interview subject fits into the story. It also helps you better control the interview so as to get the information you need. Decide the broad areas you want to cover and in what order. The order should lead logically from one topic to the next.

Working from the general to the specific within each topic you cover is effective with public figures who avoid publicly committing to specific positions or try to wriggle out of apparent wrongdoing. This strategy works best if you have enough time to conduct the interview or you restrict the interview to a narrow line of questioning. It works like a dragnet; you throw your net wide and then pull it in ever tighter to prevent escape. Here's an abbreviated version:

"Senator Sleeze, do you believe it's ethical for legislators to do special favors for constituents in exchange for campaign contributions?"

"No, of course not. Terrible. Awful. Dastardly. I believe in avoiding even the appearance of a conflict of interest. Legislators must uphold the highest ethical standards in order to maintain the integrity of the democratic process, blah, blah, blah. . . ."

"Senator, public records show that last year you accepted a million dollars from Megacorp and then just a week later sponsored legislation for a tax exemption so specific that Megacorp was the only beneficiary—to the tune of ten million bucks. Weren't you doing Megacorp a special favor in exchange for a campaign contribution?"

"Uh, well, that was actually, technically, not a campaign contribution . . . it was for my fun fund. And the timing was pure coincidence. Besides, I would have sponsored that legislation anyway. More money for Megacorp means more jobs for my constituents, blah, blah, blah. . . ."

With less experienced interview subjects and subjects of personality profiles, the general question—think of it as an essay question as opposed to the multiple-choice or true-false question—is intended to get the person talking. After all, that's primarily what you're there for: to record their words, in addition to observing them. The last thing you want from these people are yes-or-no answers, unless you're extracting facts.

Starting with specific questions and staying with them is often the best strategy, however, with children and other people who may not think in the abstract. That way they can get their minds, and thus their answers, around something concrete, say a specific incident. Whether your questions are general or specific, think of questions that will provoke revealing and informative responses, and result in vivid quotes.

Write out your questions; a half-dozen to a dozen will suffice for an hour's interview. A written list ensures that you remember important topics and specific questions. Also, line up a few more topics to discuss in case you can extend the interview.

It's OK to bring your written list to the interview; most interview subjects won't mind. They don't even have to know if you don't want them to. You can conceal your list of questions or write them in your notebook. Use your list as a guide, not a script. Don't straitjacket the interview into your prescribed interview plan. Guide the interview and make sure to hit your points, but also allow the interview to flow naturally to some extent. You'll get more from your interview subject.

Save the tough questions for last, or as Jessica Mitford also advises, order your questions from "kind to cruel." Interview subjects are more likely to answer your most probing questions at the end of an interview, if and when you've established a rapport, than at the beginning, when they're presumably more nervous about the interview per se and you as a strange interviewer. Plus, if they're going to throw you out of their office for asking unpleasant questions, it might as well be after you've asked all your other questions.

Face to Face, or Phone to Phone: The Interview Itself

As suggested in the previous section, one of the most important things you must do as an interviewer is to establish a rapport with your interview subject. Whether the interview's primary purpose is fact gathering or plumbing the depths of a personality, you won't get very far without emotionally connecting with your subject at some level. Rapport is like greasing the wheels; the words will flow, since humans as a species are a gregarious bunch, and subjects may even volunteer information that might not necessarily be in their best interest.

You build rapport with empathy. You can try to fake empathy, and there a few techniques you can employ, which I'll get to in a moment, but people can usually sense real empathy, which is a genuine, emotional identification with people's concerns and feelings. You don't have to do anything overt. Genuine empathy, even if summoned from a small part of you for a person you might actually abhor, will manifest itself in subtle ways: phrasing of questions, tone of voice, body language. Pass whatever judgments you want in print, but at the interview remain accepting of your subject and nonjudgmental, even when asking tough questions.

Empathizing with interview subjects is not the same as sucking up to them. Most professional journalists consider it exceedingly bad form to dissolve into a fan in the presence of an interview subject. In most cases, it's best to maintain some professional distance. In many ways, interview subjects, especially professional interview subjects, feel more secure with professionals; they feel they're in capable hands. They may in fact feel nervous or suspicious of sycophantic behavior.

If you truly cross the line from writer to fan, then your loyalty likewise switches from your readers and the honesty of your story to your subject. In writing your article, you'll conceal information or shade it to protect or pump up your subject undeservedly. In short, you'll become your subject's press agent. Professionalism is not necessarily a euphemism for cold and merciless. You can project genuine empathy while maintaining your professionalism.

Dressing the Part

Toward the objective of achieving professionalism with empathy, dress appropriately. People feel more comfortable with people they believe are like them in some way. Dress for the occasion, but also dress in accordance with your position as a professional there to do a job. If you're going to interview a captain of industry, dress for success. If you're going to interview a grunge rocker, leave the pinstripes at home and pull out the plaid flannel shirt. Within that context, dress the way you feel most comfortable and in a way that projects your own personal genuineness and honesty. In other words, if you're an East Coast urbanite and you're going to interview a rodeo star, don't dress and act like a cowboy. There's no better way to earn the contempt of people than to appear phony.

If all this advice about how to look and act during an interview sounds more like theater than journalism, good. Because an interview is theater of sorts. It's not simply an exchange of questions and answers. And even though it may appear to be a conversation, it is not. Experienced interview subjects are aware of this, but with your considerable interviewing talent you can make them forget. Inexperienced interview subjects are a lot easier to fool. This may sound cynical, but a hot, long-standing debate among nonfiction writers is whether writers, by doing their jobs as they supposedly should, betray their interview subjects. The full debate has consumed thousands of words, so I won't go into it here. But on the positive side, you might say, yes, but for a noble cause: to get at the unvarnished truth as you understand it after a fair evaluation of all the facts you can muster.

So now you get to the interview, punctually; you shake hands and introduce yourself again; you thank your interview subject for consenting to the interview, again; you make some brief, small talk as you set up your tape recorder; you explain to them, again, the focus of your story; you get the subject's consent to tape them and you ask them to spell their first and last name and state their birth date, presuming this is not a person whose name and birth date you should already know.

So, now, what about the questions?

Asking the Questions

Ease into the interview. In the first few minutes, you just want to warm up your interview subjects. Ask a background question or two. Then when they seem more relaxed, start in with the substantial topics, either the most important first or perhaps one or two that build to the topic of primary concern. Then follow with topics in descending order of importance.

The foregoing is a general outline, describing a typical interview in which your story is most likely a limited profile on a person or a particular aspect of that peson's life. You can cut the small talk and get right down to business when it comes to public figures talking about their public positions or experts who are basically supplying you facts and figures. They're usually busy people; they'll appreciate your just-the-facts approach.

Also, as mentioned before, save the tough questions for last, the ones, usually about illegal or immoral behavior, that might put an untimely end to the interview. You also want to wait for the right moment to ask questions that carry great emotional weight for your subject. With experience and your own excellent perception, you'll learn the right moment. And for interviews in which the subject basically recounts an episode, begin at the beginning; simply have the subject walk you through it chronologically.

Communications scholars categorize lines of questioning by their logical construction: funnel interview, in which you proceed from general ideas to specific facts, that is from essay questions to multiple-choice and true-false questions designed to elicit facts; inverted funnel interview, in which you move in the opposite direction, from specifics to generalizations or concepts; tunnel interview, basically a series of multiple-choice or true-false questions about a specific situation or incident; covertly sequenced interview, in which you try to trap people into admitting inconsistencies or wrongdoing by, for instance, first asking their position on a general concept and then later in the interview confronting them with the facts of an incident in which they were involved (the last, tough question); free-form interview, best for personality profiles in which you have sufficient time to ask essay questions that test the interview subject's intellect and character.

Obviously, some lines of questioning work better with some people than others, and most of the time you'll use combinations of them in the same interview. Remember, eventually you want to get down to specific cases with almost everyone you interview, because concrete illustrations bring ideas and concepts to life and make a story interesting.

Writer Lonny Shavelson realized how he had to switch gears in questioning a man about his reaction to his daughter's leukemia for articles and ultimately a book, *Toxic Nation*, about toxic pollution in the United States.

"I asked him how he felt when he first heard about his daughter's leukemia," Shavelson recalls. "He said he felt bad and shaken up.

These generalized emotions were the only kinds of responses I could get when I asked how he felt. So I tried to approach it another way. I asked, 'Where were you when you first heard about it?' He then told me the whole story starting with him first coming out of the shower and his wife calling him to the phone. So I went from him feeling bad to this scene of a nearly naked man almost falling to the floor in his kitchen. Then I didn't have to tell the reader that he felt bad. It was obvious."

As you can see from Shavelson's example, sometimes you must ask concrete questions to get concrete answers. An academic may prefer to theorize, so ask about the specific physical and mental acts that lead to the theory. Children and people without much formal education tend to think in specifics, so skip the concept questions, such as asking a six-year-old, "Do you think the violence in Saturday morning TV cartoons plays a direct role in violence among children?" Answer: "Dunno." First try questions that ask who, what, where and when, which are multiple-choice questions, followed by "how" and "why" essay questions.

"How" and "why" questions work well with just about everyone for eliciting extended responses, because essentially they're asking for explanations. Those kinds of questions will often induce a subject to tell you an anecdote, which is just what you need for enlivening your story. Also, ask people directly to give you an example. Questions containing superlatives also work well for eliciting personality profile anecdotes: What's your favorite/least favorite . . . When was the first/ last time you . . . What was your best/worst. . . . A favorite of celebrity interviewer Barbara Walters: "When was the last time you cried?"

Ask clear, concise questions, not multiple-part questions, which can confuse the subject. Break the multiple-part question down and ask each part one at a time.

Don't be afraid to appear naive; it's your prerogative as a journalist. Remember, you represent the typical reader of the publication for which you're targeting your story. People in almost any field—be it law or medicine, nuclear physics, personnel management or dog training— often answer questions as though they're speaking to a colleague. They may speak in jargon and at a level of expertise no one reasonably expects readers to possess. Sometimes they do it innocently, because their job is not, after all, communication; sometimes they do it because it's easier than explaining it to you; sometimes they do it because they themselves aren't sure of the answer and they're covering up their ignorance; and sometimes they do it to impress or intimidate you with their knowledge. Have none of it. Insist on your ignorance, politely and self-effacingly. Ask them to please explain it to you. And repeat it back to them in your own words. Better to appear stupid in front of your interview subject than get it wrong and appear stupid in print.

There's only so far, however, that you can take the journalistic license of ignorance. First, you should possess the same level of expertise as your readers. So if you're interviewing a lawyer for *Litigation Daily*, you should be conversant with basic legal terms and procedures. Also, sometimes in the case of busy, important people, you often can get background information and explanations from underlings. And then there are the truly dumb questions: "And just what is it you do for a living, Mr. Sinatra?"

Related to the dumb question is the question to which you already know the answer or to which you're almost certain of the answer. This is a legitimate question. The point nearly every time is to get the subject's response on the record or to confirm on the record previously published facts and opinions. As you might have figured, I'm talking about controversy. The subject may deny making certain statements or the veracity of published facts.

Remember, however, just because subjects tell you something is true or false about themselves doesn't mean they're telling the truth. A good journalistic rule is to assume nothing. That's why you ask the question to which you already know the answer. Preface your question with a reference to previously published works to let the subject know that you've done your homework and are not merely asking a dumb question.

Once you've asked your question, make sure you let your subject answer. Believe or not, people tend to cut other people off when they're talking, or start talking the moment the other person quits. Pause before asking the next question. And for questions to which you want more than simple facts, leave some dead space after the answer. People naturally want to fill the awkward silences in conversations, so interview subjects often elaborate on their initial answers to fill the void.

There are times in the interview when voicing declarative sentences rather than questions can help you. To build rapport, go ahead and share a (very encapsulated) personal story of your own if you think it will encourage a subject to continue talking about an emotional topic. But tell no I-can-top-that-one stories: The point is to demonstrate your empathy with them, not to one-up them. The opposite gambit works occasionally, but it's risky. Sometimes if you spill your guts, people feel they have to respond in kind. You can also encourage interview subjects to keep talking, especially when telling an anecdote, with the typical "uh huhs" and "yeses" of conventional conversation that essentially say, "Yes, I'm listening."

As your interview draws to a close, keep in mind a few stock questions intended to catch odds and ends. First, if it's relevant, ask about the interview subject's plans for the future if you haven't already done so. Then ask if there's anyone else they'd recommend you talk to, and finally ask if there's anything else they'd like to add or any areas you haven't covered. You'd be surprised at the responses you'll get. These last questions about future plans and anything else to add can induce the interview subject to launch into whole new areas you hadn't even thought about, or to spill a confession. Also, somewhere in there thank them for their time and ask if you may contact them again with follow-up questions to ensure fairness and accuracy.

So now, the interview's over, right? Not quite. Invariably, after the formal interview ends, the interview subject, and you, too, relax. You step out of your roles as journalist and interview subject, and become normal people again. You'll find people often want to chat some more at this point, person to person, and so once again, like that first moment of contact, be prepared for a great quote to come your way. Keep your cassette recorder running on your way out the door, or scribble down that quotable gem as the door shuts behind you.

Using (or Not Using) Quotes

Just because someone said something and you've got it on tape doesn't mean you have to quote them verbatim. In fact, professional nonfiction writers rarely quote anyone verbatim. People speak elliptically, and they interject lots of superfluous words and, well, animal noises in their speech. They say, "like" and "you know," and they utter, "um, uh, huh, hum" and "hmm." So, it's perfectly acceptable to clean up people's quotes, and you shouldn't not clean up their quotes just to make them look stupid in print.

In selecting quotes, choose the phrases and sentences that best convey a person's unique personality or describe a situation in colorful terms. Use quotes from each interview subject sparingly and judiciously in most stories for greatest impact. Such quotes are the sentence or few sentences in what may have been a five-minute monologue that speak to the emotional or intellectual heart of the matter. Obviously, you typically quote key players more often than supporting players or commentators. For stories in which one or a few specific facts are paramount and, usually, controversial—in other words, they are the story—then quote the source for the record to fortify your printed claim of the fact and its source.

There are times when you'll interview sources and agree not to quote them by name, or at all, or not even to write any of the information they give you. You've probably heard of the following journalistic terms: off the record, on background, not for attribution. As the terms are imprecise, journalists and sources often have varying definitions of these terms, so if you or a source use them spell out exactly your agreement.

In general the terms are defined as follow: "off the record" means you agree not to publish the information even if you get it from another source, or you can publish it if you get it from another source (definitions vary, the latter is sometimes called deep background); "on background" means you can use the information but not quote or identify the source in any way (this might lead you to a source who will grant at least limited attribution); "not for attribution" means you can use the information, even quotes, but not identify the source by name or some way that would otherwise specify identity, therefore a limited, general attribution, such as the frequently used "a White House source," is allowed.

As you can see, you give up your freedom to publish openly information you've gathered by agreeing to any restrictive terms. Reporters do agree to them, however, in the hopes of gaining more important information, or at least reporting some information rather than none at all. Sometimes reporters agree to partially withhold information to have at least some information with which to beat the competition; they take a bribe of sorts in exchange for their silence. Give up as little as possible. And don't be seduced by sources who want to make you feel like an insider by sharing secrets with you that you can't use.

If you've identified yourself as a journalist and you agree to none of the foregoing restrictive terms, then the interview is understood to be "on the record." In other words, you are free to print whatever you're told within the bounds of libel laws and, possibly, your own good taste. Occasionally, interview subjects, after blabbing unthinkingly, will think better of it and protest that they didn't realize their comments were for publication. Ignore this ploy.

Along those lines, resist allowing a subject or source to review your story before publication. It's bad journalistic practice because it's fraught with all kinds of danger for your journalistic integrity. The subject can possibly pressure you, your editor or the publisher into changing the story so that the story no longer represents your perspective, but rather the subject's. Unfortunately, in their lust for celebrity interviews, some magazines have relinquished varying degrees of editorial control to their celebrity subjects.

It is perfectly acceptable, however, to double-check facts and even quotes with a subject. That doesn't mean you are obliged to change whatever your interview subject or source tells you to. You must judge whether your subject misspoke innocently or made a factual error the first time around. As for quotes, you simply must decide which quote is most honest to your story. Sometimes, in controversial situations, a reporter might insert conflicting quotes in the story and explain the circumstances under which they were made.

Tools of the Trade

For some time, professional nonfiction writers have debated which is the better technique for interviewing: taking notes or using a tape recorder. As journalists are human, despite the persistent myth to the contrary (something about them being vultures), they, like everyone else, take the easy way out. Which is why, despite the ravings of the neo-Luddites in the press corps, the tape recorder, or more precisely the cassette or microcassette recorder, has become standard equipment for interviewing. It's a lot easier to let the recorder pick up every sound the subject utters than to scribble it all down furiously. Let's consider other, more substantial advantages of tape-recording interviews:

1. *Recording is accurate.* Writing down what people say cannot compete with a machine, when it's working, which leads directly to point number two.

2. *Recording provides proof of the interview subject's own words.* Subjects too often claim, untruthfully, that they've been misquoted, usually when their printed words get them into trouble. A taped recording all but eliminates this problem. With their exact words on tape, you quote them accurately *and* you have proof you quoted them accurately. They're left only with the claim that you quoted them "out of context," a much weaker claim. Perhaps you've noticed the phrase, "out of context," is now preferred over "misquoted" by public figures who injudiciously shoot from the lip. That's because many journalists now use tape recorders.

3. *Recording improves the flow of the interview.* Writing notes often slows down the interview when the interview subject pauses or speaks slower so you can catch up. This can break the subject's speech patterns and speaking rhythm, and break the intimate atmosphere you've worked so hard to establish.

4. *Recording improves the interview's direction.* You can better concentrate on asking the next question or set of questions, think about the next logical topic to cover and gauge how well the interview is going.

5. *Recording improves the interaction between the interviewer and interview subject.* You can better engage the interview subject with more eye-to-eye contact and a more natural interaction. This makes the interview appear more like a conversation, and so less formal, which helps you establish rapport with your subject.

6. *Recording gives you more opportunity to observe the subject.* The subject's tone of voice, speech patterns, gestures and body language are also important to your understanding of your subject, and you may want to include your observations of these characteristics in your story. You can also better observe the surroundings.

7. *Recording can improve your interviewing skills.* You can learn a lot by listening to your own participation in the interview, such as whether you failed to pursue a line of questioning or talked too much or too little.

Many journalists who use cassette recorders during interviews also take notes at the same time. Why? Because journalists, like people and vultures, respond to fear—the horrifying, machine malfunction potential the neo-Luddites like to cite.

So taking notes provides some insurance (I suppose you could use two recorders). But taking notes in conjunction with recording provides a few additional advantages. It's easier to find key quotes when listening to the tape if you've made a note of them during the interview or generally noted the course of the interview. You can also note the number on the tape counter if you can place the recorder close enough to the subject for the mike to pick up the sound and close enough to you so you can see the counter. Also, it's easier to find stated facts in your notebook than listening to the tape and then writing down the facts again. In addition, you'll undoubtedly want to make written notes of your observations relating to your other four senses. Getting down a person's words is only a component, albeit usually the most important component, of an interview.

To help improve your chances that your tape recorder won't mess up on you, test it before going to the interview and make sure that you have fresh batteries in it. Buy a recorder with that uses AC and DC currents so that you can plug it into the wall, thereby bypassing the batteries completely. (Here's another consumer tip: A recorder with a "remote" jack allows you to plug a handheld mike into the recorder or a foot pedal for transcribing.) If you do plug the recorder in, turn it on to make sure the outlet works. In any event, check to see that the tape is moving when you start the interview, and check on it occasionally throughout the interview if you can.

If you go the recording route, make sure your interview subject consents *on tape* to being taped. In some states it's illegal to tape record people without their consent, and you want to make sure you have documented proof of their consent. Try to do it as friendly and officiously as possible, but do it. Start off stating on tape that the following is a taped interview with a certain person on a certain date, and then ask again (since you've asked before pulling out the tape recorder and turning it on) if it's OK to tape them. Since with most interview subjects you'll want to confirm the spelling of their name, first and last, now's the best time to ask them to spell it.

To give the neo-Luddites their due, there are a few strong arguments against tape-recording interviews. Someone has to transcribe the tape, a time-consuming effort, and that someone will probably be you unless you can afford to pay someone else to do it. Barring transcription, you still have to listen to the whole interview again to get the quotes you want. If you're on a tight deadline, as newspaper reporters often are, and you're after only a few short quotes from an incidental source, it's probably easier just to jot down some notes.

The anti-recorder crowd also contends that interview subjects choke at the sight of a cassette recorder. It brings home to them concretely that you plan to enshrine their words in print, and they're afraid their own words will make them appear foolish. (Many veteran interviewers counter that interview subjects quickly forget about the recorder.) They also point to any machine's fallibility; it can malfunction despite your preinterview sound test, and you might not even be aware of it. When you get back to your office and play back the tape, you find all those great quotes have evaporated into thin air.

In addition to tape recorders, modern technology has given writers another way to record interviews: the laptop computer. There's no extra transcribing time involved, yet you can get a much more complete and accurate record of the interview than by taking notes, assuming that you type quicker than you write. Like taking notes, however, your eyes are pretty much confined to your screen, and the preoccupying act of typing the subject's words distances you from the subject. That might be just fine if you're interviewing a securities analyst about movements in the bond market, but not so fine for an interview with the survivor of a train wreck or a broken marriage. The cost of an extra computer might understandably exceed a freelance writer's budget, but given the computing power of the newest laptops, many people have turned to laptops as their only computer.

Field Research

Through your article, which is a written interpretation of your research, you guide your readers to an understanding of your subject. When you interview people, you represent your readers' emotions and intellect. And in observing your story in real life, that is, out in the field, you serve as your readers' surrogate eyes and ears—and nose, skin and taste buds.

You've probably heard the expression, God is in the details (or alternatively, the devil is in the details). However you want to put it, the point is if you speak or write in generalities you'll never get to the core of an issue, to a deep understanding of it, and your story will never come to life. As mentioned in the section on interviewing, that's the value of anecdotes: to illustrate a concept, to make concrete the abstract. And the more vivid your anecdote the more effective it is. What makes an anecdote vivid? Details. A lot of little, but telling, details. Up to a point, the more details, the more concrete your anecdote.

It's better in a landscape description, for instance, to write that "a thick forest of conifers covered the valley floor" than "a thick forest covered the valley floor." The reader instantly visualizes a mass of evergreens. Better yet, write that "a thick forest of spruce and pine covered the valley floor." That's even more specific. But first, of course, when you're out in the field, you have to observe what kind of trees make up the forest.

You also have to know when to stop. Is it really better to write that "a thick forest of Englemann's spruce and lodgepole pine" covered the valley floor? Probably not, unless your story has something to do with Englemann. It also depends on your readers. How knowledgeable are they in the subject? How interested are they in certain details? You might want to describe a forest of pine trees as lodgepole and sugar pines to readers of *High Country Monthly* but perhaps not to readers of *High Living*.

It seems obvious to say that all our observations come to us through our five senses (for those of us who exist in only three dimensions), but you wouldn't know it from reading the many articles in which place plays a prominent role. Writers often convey a sense of place through the one or two senses most strongly developed within themselves. You will undoubtedly rely on sight more than any other sense; "sight" observations invariably outnumber the observations from any other sense because the eyes can record more distinct, individual and describable items than other senses. But the judicious use of other sensory observations gives readers a full, multidimensional sense of a place. For example, keeping in mind the timeworn dictum for good writing, "show don't tell," it's much more effective describe a warm climate by writing that your skin felt clammy and your damp clothes clung to your skin than it is to write that the weather was hot and humid.

To capture the full array of sensory details, you must consciously and continually take note of all five senses, which is no small task. Smell, especially, is an overlooked sense; smells often evoke memories. Taste is also a powerful but overlooked sense. I know a writer who specializes in the culinary aspects of travel. This approach, which necessarily involves the senses of both taste and smell, gives him a distinct advantage in bringing a locale to life.

Details that add meaning to a story are often called "significant details," a self-explanatory phrase. Tom Wolfe, whose work focuses on American society, additionally uses the phrase "status detail" to describe the kinds of details that reveal a person's social status: the clothes a person wears, the house and car, but particularly specific objects, maybe a writing pen, that speak volumes about a person's social status, lifestyle and attitudes.

Keeping in mind, however, that significant details raise an article to a higher level of quality, you can no more be indiscriminate with your sensory details than with your statistical and documentary details. The best details not only give readers a sense of place but also inject a greater meaning in your article. Whether symbolic or literal, they support the article's theme.

To illustrate how a skillful writer uses significant and status details, let's examine an article in my hometown alternative weekly newspaper, *East Bay Express*. The article, by Laura Hagar, is about Richard Ofshe, the U.C. Berkeley professor who is controversial for disputing recovered memories of childhood sexual abuse.

In the article, Ofshe is about to give a reading at a Berkeley bookstore, and he knows he's facing a largely hostile audience. Hagar states that Ofshe is a man who relishes a fight, and this is how she illustrates it: "While most authors huddle in the back room waiting to be introduced, he [Ofshe] stood confidently, almost cockily in the midst of the crowd gathered at the entrance. Ofshe didn't exactly swagger, but then he didn't need to—his smile, the set of his shoulders, the look in his eyes as they swept the room did the swaggering for him."

The adverb "cockily" is more specific than "confidently," and even more specific are the descriptions of his smile, shoulders and eyes. They are concrete, significant details that convincingly reveal Ofshe's personality.

Later in the piece, she mentions that a *New Yorker* article about recovered memory described Ofshe as resembling Zeus. In that light, and to support her characterization of Ofshe as a powerful, authoritative figure, she describes his house (she had also described him physically) thusly:

"There is also something Olympian about his house, set high above the city. . . . His new house, which he helped design, is a dramatic, multi-level, neo-Tuscan affair with hand-sponged walls, daring geometric elements, and a breathtaking, pulse-racing floor-to-ceiling window overlooking the canyon. A red-tailed hawk spiraled past the window as we spoke."

Some of this description is not description but exposition: "something Olympian about his house," referring to the house as "dramatic," the elements "daring," and the view "breathtaking, pulse-racing." Yet, there's enough concrete description to support the assertions: "his house, set high above the city," "multi-level, neo-Tuscan affair," "hand-sponged walls," "geometric elements," "floor-to-ceiling window overlooking the canyon."

Since Hagar's article is, after all, about Ofshe and not his house, she refrains from indulging in too much description. For instance, "geometric" is an imprecise adjective, but Hagar would have strayed too far from her subject, Ofshe, and her purpose, using the house as a tangible representation of Ofshe's personality, had she gone into the triangles and rectangles of Ofshe's house.

Notice particularly Hagar's mention that Ofshe helped design the house. This small fact supports Hagar's claims for Ofshe's considerable mental powers, an important element in Hagar's thesis that Ofshe is correct in claiming that therapists' recovered memory assertions are often fraudulent. It appears Hagar made small talk with Ofshe about his home. She may have asked whether he helped design it, but more likely he volunteered the information in response to her interest. Some curiosity and questions that digress briefly from the immediate subject can prove fruitful.

The bit about the red-tailed hawk spiraling past the window is a nice touch. It does seem to place Hagar's Zeus (Ofshe) on Olympus, and the hawk resonates with Hagar's previous description of Ofshe's strong personality.

As a last word, keep in mind that people adapt to their surroundings; it's a basic survival skill. What was once extraordinary becomes ordinary. So when in the field, keep reminding yourself that what has become commonplace to you is still new and exciting to your readers. They can only come along for the ride via your five senses, and essentially only once and for a short time, when they read your story. With nonfiction, you can't make up the details, you must observe them. You'll often get only one chance to observe a significant detail, and it will occur in a split second. That's why you must maintain a high degree of alertness to observe people and places successfully.

This is how fiction writer Eudora Welty explained how her job as a photographer for the Works Progress Administration during the Depression taught her to be prepared for the telling moment in the field:

"It had more than information and accuracy to teach me. I learned in the doing how *ready* I had to be. Life doesn't hold still. . . . Photography taught me that to be able to capture transience, by being ready to click the shutter at the crucial moment, was the greatest need I had. Making pictures of people in all sorts of situations, I learned that every feeling waits upon its gesture; and I had to be prepared to recognize this moment when I saw it. These were things a story writer needed to know."

CHAPTER EIGHT

Evaluating Research: Some Closing Thoughts

To know anything well involves a profound sensation of ignorance.—John Ruskin

The public demands . . . certainties. . . . But there are no certainties.—H.L. Mencken

You've researched your story for days, maybe weeks. You've searched through every book, magazine article, report and survey you can get your hands on. You've talked to everyone you can possibly think of. You've amassed a mountain of information. You've got so much information you're overwhelmed by it. You don't know how to order it into a comprehensible form, and worse, you don't even know what it means. You're staring into a pit of chaos.

If your story's big, complex and multifaceted, there's no easy way to make sense of it; this, after all, is the heaviest mental lifting the writer faces. But if you live with your material long enough, way less than a lifetime in most cases, then it will start to make sense to you. You'll begin to connect the dots.

The science fiction writer Ray Bradbury expressed such sentiments years ago during a lecture in Los Angeles. He said he steeped himself in his material before beginning to write, and ideas percolated up from his subconscious. Then he understood the deeper meaning of his work and began to write.

Before I begin to write, I follow Bradbury's advice. I read over my notes, maybe two or three times, not only to organize them but to fix the information in my mind as much as possible. I don't mean I try to memorize everything, but rather I familiarize myself with the material once it's assembled. I like to tape interviews and transcribe them because the process of listening and writing helps me learn my subject similar to the way one listens to tapes to learn a foreign language.

As you think about your story, make more notes of the notes you made during your initial information gathering. Ask additional questions, comment on information, evaluate the usefulness of information, note ideas that pop into your head and jot them down immediately. Pay particular attention to general concepts and salient points. Look for larger and deeper meanings beyond the obvious ones. Think about your story even if you think you understand it. Have second, third, even fourth thoughts about your story.

Don't worry if you can't make sense of your material right away; you need to walk around with your story for awhile. With the benefit of time, thoughts begin to ricochet inside your head and collide, making connections. Themes and patterns emerge as if by magic. Your thoughts reach critical mass. The fog lifts; the story becomes clear.

INDEX